SPECIAL DIET COOKBOOKS
LOW~FAT & NO~FAT
COOKING

A varied collection of sugar-free, wholefood recipes for those who
need to reduce their fat intake for medical reasons or for those who
simply want to shape up.

SPECIAL DIET COOKBOOKS
LOW~FAT & NO~FAT
COOKING

Jackie Applebee

Illustrated by Ian Jones

THORSONS PUBLISHING GROUP

First published 1984
Second edition 1989

British Library Cataloguing in Publication Data

Applebee, Jackie
Low-fat and no-fat cooking. 2nd ed.
1. Low-fat diet — Recipes
I. Title
641.5'638   RM237.7

ISBN 0-7225-2207-X

Published by Thorsons Publishers Limited,
Wellingborough, Northamptonshire, NN8 2RQ, England

Printed and bound in Great Britain by
Mackays of Chatham PLC, Chatham, Kent

3 5 7 9 10 8 6 4

CONTENTS

PREFACE

I have written this book by using the basic principles that we use in teaching wholefood cooking. All of the recipes are sugar-free, only natural sweeteners in the form of fresh and dried fruit, honey, malt, molasses or rice syrup are used.

Various grains are used, but they are all wholegrains or flours made from whole grains. Hopefully in our recipes, especially when making bread and pastry, we have guided you to look at the texture of your food instead of quoting strict quantities of liquid to be used in the various dishes. This is most important, as you can appreciate, dealing and handling natural foods you are sure to get variants.

In teaching I use as little dairy produce as possible and this book gave me a good opportunity to use foods that are becoming easily available or are simple to make, for example tofu, which is a soya bean curd; okara, the by-product of tofu; seitan, a food made from washing wheat and many more foods easily available in most wholefood shops.

To write a low-fat cook book was a pleasure, as we have too much fat in our diet, but to write a no-fat cook book was a challenge and, I hope, an aid to the many people who, through ill-health, have to have a low or non-fat diet.

JACKIE APPLEBEE

1.
WHY DO WE NEED A <u>LITTLE</u> FAT?

Whether fat is saturated or unsaturated, two-fifths of the fat in most British diets is undisguised. It takes the form of salad oil, butter, mayonnaise, etc. Then there are the hidden fats in meat, milk, dairy produce, convenience foods, pastry, cream, sauces, nuts and so on. Vegetables and plant products contain considerably less or no fat.

However a little fat in the diet is necessary because it contains an essential nutrient which is a polyunsaturated acid called linoleic acid. Other fatty acids can be synthesized by the body if linoleic acid is present, but we cannot synthesize linoleic acid. Only 1.2 per cent of our total calorific requirement is linoleic acid — this is approximately one tablespoonful per day.

It is well known that over-consumption of fat causes cardiovascular disease, of which heart attack and stroke are examples. Research consistently points to the risk factors of fat-like substances in the blood called cholesterol, and high blood-pressure coupled with too little exercise, a diet too rich in saturated fat, diabetes and 'hurry sickness'. In any combination of two or three factors all of these things aggravate each other.

Fat serves several purposes in the body. These functions are performed by the fact that fats and water do not mix, so the fatty tissue of the body can store and transport other substances like fat soluble vitamins which otherwise would not be carried by the blood. This also means the fat cannot be dissolved by body fluids — so it is an excellent energy reserve. Fat within the body is used for fuel; upon digesting it, it produces twice as much energy as the equal weight of carbohydrate or protein. On eating a good diet the energy reserve should be continually used and replaced. This is governed by the correct calorific intake, thus bringing about no weight gain. The balance is essential to good health.

The Western World diet provides people with approximately 40 per cent of calories from fat. This is an excessive amount and we have taken this fact into account by writing a cookery book with recipes containing very little or no fat. Very little fat is necessary for nourishment as so many foods contain natural fats.

Every cook can appreciate the qualities of fat in cooking; it has the ability to absorb flavour — this is why people on a low - fat diet and who want to lose weight should beware of convenience foods. Make sure that the food has not been coated with margarine, this automatically makes the food satisfying, but because of the high proportion of calories, the foods take longer to digest and the stomach stays fuller longer.

There are three different types of fat found within food:
1. Saturated
2. Mono-unsaturated
3. Polyunsaturated
This is determined by the make up of the individual food's fatty acid chains.

Structurally a fatty acid is a chain of carbon atoms each with hydrogen atoms attached. Fatty acids with four or more hydrogen atoms missing are called polyunsaturated fatty acids (*Polyunsaturates*); these have been found to lower the blood cholesterol.

Cholesterol is part of the body structure and a normal constituent of the bloodstream. It is needed for all membranes — particularly nerves and also for the synthesis of some hormones, bile salts and vitamin D. People living in Western societies tend to accumulate cholesterol and, as a result, the amount circulating in the bloodstream often rises with increasing age.

Saturated Fats
These tend to be fats high in cholesterol and are found in such foods

as milk, butter, eggs and meat. Beware of some margarines as despite the labelling 'high in polyunsaturates' they often contain a percentage of saturated fat.

Mono-unsaturated Fats

This term refers to foods that contain at least one double bond, those containing more being called polyunsaturated. Foods containing mono-unsaturated fat are avocado pear, olive oil, coconut oil, and should be eaten in the diet in moderation

Polyunsaturated Fats

These are oils with multiple double bonding and are used by the body for breaking down the unsaturated fatty acids. Unsaturated oils distribute the fat-soluble vitamins around the body, supply energy, conserve body heat, build new tissues and promote the growth of beneficial intestinal bacteria. They also help in the breakdown of saturated fats in the body. Oils that contain polyunsaturated fatty acids are corn oil, safflower, sunflower and sesame oil. Most vegetable and plant products contain polyunsaturated fat, e.g. grains, beans, seeds, etc.

The easiest and most apparent difference is that saturated fats are usually solid at room temperature, for example butter and lard and unsaturated fats are liquid oil. Margarine serves to be the exception to this rule, but margarine starts its life as oil and through various processes becomes a solid fat. In wholefood terms margarine is a highly processed food and we do not use it at all. The recipes in this book will only contain cold-pressed oil and for those on a fat-free diet we have substituted fat in a lot of our recipes by using *okara*. This is made by processing soya beans and using the fibre and pulp only of the beans.

Cold-pressed Oils

This term refers of the method of processing the oil from the nut, vegetable or seed. It is quite easy to recognize cold-pressed oil as the aroma should be of its extraction and so, therefore, cold-pressed sesame seed oil should smell of sesame seeds. Only 35% of the oil is extracted from the original nut, vegetable or seed by cold-pressing it in comparison to 74% extraction if pressed by commercial means.

It is the nutritional value of the oil that is lost in manufacture and often harmful substances are added during extraction and refining. Oils can be extracted from vegetable origin by mechanical pressing or by the use of chemical solvents. There are two methods used in mechanical extraction, the traditional method being that of simply pressing the food with a hydraulic press. The oil then has to be filtered and is ready for use. The actual process produces a little heat, but not enough to destroy the vitamins and minerals in the oil. This method only suits soft seeds, e.g. olive, sesame and sunflower. Safflower and corn are too hard for this method to be used, so they are pressed by the use of a screw or expeller press. This exerts more force than a hydraulic press. The food used for extraction is also steamed prior to the pressing. In comparison the rate of extraction by the above two methods is much lower than that of commercial extraction.

When oil is extracted commercially, the oil-bearing materials are ground, steamed and then mixed with solvents (usually petroleum based, such as benzene, hexane or heptane). The mixture is then heated to drive off the solvent. After this the oils go through a refining process which consists of washing the oil with caustic soda. This removes the lecithin from the oil. It is then bleached and filtered through a fine sieve. This removes the minerals and coloured substances. Refined oils are normally labelled 'pure', referring to 'purely refined'.

The obvious answer is not to eat too much fat at all. Cut out as much fat as possible and concentrate on the fat that is contained in whole, natural food. This provides a natural limit to your fat intake in a good tasting package which retains the flavour as well as goodness like fat-soluble vitamins, many of which are lost when oils are refined.

Common food sources of fat:

Animal sources
Whole milk   Bacon

Plant sources
Vegetables oils — corn, cotton, peanut

Animal sources		*Plant sources*	
Butter	Cheese	Mayonnaise	Salad dressing
Lard	Cream	Chocolate	Peanut butter
Meat fats	Egg yolk	Nuts	Avocados
		Olives	Coconuts

The various oils serve completely different purposes in cooking and preparing food by their flavour, colour and texture. For cakes, biscuits, puddings and sweet dishes, cold-pressed corn oil or sunflower oil is best suited, whereas sesame and peanut oil are excellent in savoury dishes. For cold dishes that are also savoury, olive oil and mustard oil are well suited. Safflower cold-pressed oil is an excellent oil as it is suited to every cooking purpose and it is a polyunsaturated oil. I am reluctant to use soya oil having never been able to obtain a cold-pressed variety, but is is a good medium for oiling tins and dishes.

The nutritive value of the cold-pressed oils is much higher than manufactured oils but in relation to this the price is much higher. This equates itself in that you use far less cold-pressed oil when cooking as it is much thicker and thins very readily when heat is applied. So if you have to use fat, for health's sake, use cold-pressed oils.

Oiling Tins
Always brush oil into a tin, you use very little oil and it saves a lot of time.

2.

BEFORE YOU START

The tofu used is 'regular tofu' and not the silken variety in the long life packaging. The former is usually sold loose or vacuum packed and it is much harder than the commercial substance. Silken tofu is much softer than the regular type because in the making it is not pressed to the same extent.

Okara is a side product of tofu and although it is not generally available soya beans are, and it is only made from these and water. Seitan is also easily made from flour and water. It is a most versatile food that can replace any type of minced meat in everyday recipes.

Vegetables should be sautéed in water wherever possible but if oil is required this can be applied by means of a brush so that an excess is avoided.

Agar: A powder made from ground seaweed, it has a gelatinous nature.

Arame: A seaweed reconstituted by placing in water.

Baking powder: Commercial baking powder kills the vitamin B in whole grains, so we tend to use *sodium-free baking powder*.

Barleycup: A grain drink.

Buckwheat: A grain also known as Kasha.

Buckwheat spaghetti: Also known as Soba.

Bulgar: Cracked roasted wheat.

Cold-pressed oil: This item refers to the type of manufacture of the oil from the original seed. It is superior in nutritive value to ordinary oil.

Dhokla: A flour made of millet and rice flour.

Gram: The name given to beans ground into flour.

Gomasio: Sesame seed salt.

Green lentils: Whole lentils, sometimes called continental lentils.

Haricot beans: A small white kidney shaped bean, better known to most people as the bean used in baked beans.

Kudzu: An arrowroot-type flour obtained from a plant tuber.

Masala dal: A collection of spices prepared for dal — a lentil dish — easily available from Asian food shops.

Miso: A paste made from fermented soya beans. *Never boil* miso as it destroys all of the micro-organisms found in it.

Mustard: A seed that can be made into a condiment by soaking for 7 days in cider vinegar. Half of the mixture is then ground or liquidized. Both seeds are then mixed together.

Okara: The fibre and the bulk left over from making soya milk or tofu.

Red lentils: Lentils that have had the outer layer removed — they are the easiest to cook of all pulses.

Rice syrup: A mild, sticky, honey-type liquid that is not at all sweet. Made from sprouted rice.

Sea salt: Salt processed from the sea. It is much lower in sodium than rock or table salt.

Seaweed: Available from most wholefood shops. Seaweeds have all 14 minerals that the body requires. A lot are lost when reconstituting seaweed in water. This is why it is just as important to use the water as well as the seaweed.

Shoyu: Soya sauce made from fermenting soya beans — do not confuse it with commercial soya sauce that contains sugar and monosodium glutamate.

Sodium-free baking powder: is made from: ⅓ arrowroot; ⅓ cream of tartar; ⅓ potassium bicarbonate.

Soya flour: Flour made from soya beans. It should always be cooked in dishes or toasted if eaten raw, to kill the trypsin inhibitor within the bean.

Tahini: Sesame seed spread — available in light or dark varieties — I suggest you use light tahini in the recipes.

Tofu: A soya bean curd. Regular tofu is a hard tofu, silken tofu is much softer.

Turmeric: Used for its yellow/orange colouring and is a member of the ginger family.

Salt, Gomasio and Salty Flavours
Salt is purely a flavouring in food and is optional at any time.

Sea Salt — this is a natural salt much lower in sodium that any of the table or rock salts you can buy.

Miso — also a digestive aid, it has a salty flavour and is used in many recipes in place of salt.

Shoyu — a soya sauce that, like miso, has a salty flavour.

Gomasio — sesame seed salt made from roasting 11 parts sesame seeds (this could be 11 teaspoonsful or 11 tablespoonsful or, if you really like it, 11 cupsful of sesame seeds) to one equal part of sea salt and grinding them together.

Seaweed — when soaking seaweed it loses 30% of the minerals into the water and this is why you should never throw away the water. The soaking water is quite salty and can be used in place of salt when making bread and pastry.

Okara
1. Soak the soya beans in plenty of water overnight.

2. Place the soaked beans in a liquidizer with fresh water and liquidize until the bean particles are quite small.

3. Place the largest saucepan you have on the stove with at least 2¼ litres of water. Bring this to the boil.

4. When the water is boiling, add the ground soya beans — this is called 'go'.

5. When the liquid starts to boil it will rise up the pan, rather like milk boiling. Have a dish of water ready and let the mixture rise; when it starts, flick it with cold water and the liquid will then die down.

6. Boil the 'go' three times and flick water on it three times.
   This is essential to get rid of the flatulence in the soya beans
   and kill any trypsin inhibitor that may be present.

7. You will need a fine sieve or muslin for the next stage.

8. Strain the 'go' through the muslin. This will give you a
   cream-coloured milk. This is soya milk and the solid is
   called *okara*.
   Okara is used in many dishes in this book. It has the texture
   of nuts without the fat content of nuts. It is high in fibre
   and low in calories.

Seitan

Seitan is made from wholewheat and can be used in dishes minced
or sliced wherever meat is used in recipes.

Home-made Seitan

Make a ball of stiff dough with wholemeal flour and water. I find
the easiest way of controlling the making of seitan is by washing it
in a large plastic colander. When you have made the ball of dough,
place it in the colander. Place it under running water and wash it
(it seems a little odd, but if you can cast your mind back to breadmaking
and pastrymaking, it is quite surprising to see large pieces of dough
intact at the end of washing up). At one stage when washing the dough
it will appear to fall apart, keep squeezing it and it will stay together.
Once all the starch has been washed out of the dough — seitan is left.
I find it much easier to use seitan if it is left to stand in the refrigerator
for a couple of hours or overnight before using. As it stands so more
water comes out of it and it becomes firm enough to be cut into small
pieces or minced — 14 oz (350g) of flour will give you approximately
½ lb (200g) seitan.
   The seitan is made from the gluten, wheatgerm and bran in the
wheat, certainly not a food for gluten-free diets.

Preparation of Tins

It is advisable to oil all bakeware including non-stick tins before use.

For plain, creamed and melted method cakes, oil and line the bottom of tin with oiled greaseproof paper.

For breads, whisked sponges and rich fruit cakes line the base and sides of tin.

Square and oblong tins.

Figure 1.

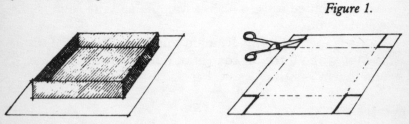

On greaseproof paper, pencil round base of tin. Fold along lines and cut as shown (Figure 1). Fit into oiled tin (Figure 2). Brush lining with oil.

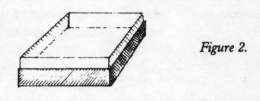

Figure 2.

Round tins.

Figure 3.

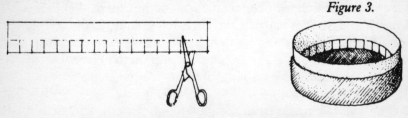

Cut a long strip of greaseproof paper to fit round tin. Fold up ½ in. (1cm) along bottom edge cut as shown (Figure 3). Place inside oiled tin so that cut edge fits around base. Cut a circle of paper for the base and fit into tin. Brush lining with oil.

3.
SOUPS, DIPS AND SPREADS

CHICK PEA SOUP
There are endless variations of this recipe.

Imperial (Metric)	American
½ lb (225g) chick peas	1 cupful garbanzo beans
4 oz (115g) brown rice	½ cupful brown rice
1 lb (455g) parsnips, scrubbed and chopped	1 pound parsnips, scrubbed and chopped
1 lb (455g) celery, chopped	1 pound celery, chopped
1 lb (455g) onions, chopped	1 pound onions, chopped
4 oz (115g) tahini	½ cupful tahini
2 teaspoonsful garam masala	2 teaspoonsful garam masala
2 teaspoonsful shoyu soya sauce, or more to taste	2 teaspoonsful shoyu soy sauce, or more to taste
2-4 pints (1¼-2½ litres) water or stock	5-10 cupsful water or stock

1. Soak the chick peas (garbanzo beans) and grain overnight and cook together until almost tender, e.g. 20 minutes in a pressure cooker.

2. Add the vegetables and finish cooking.

3. To thicken, if required, liquidize a cupful of the soup and return to the pan.

4. Heat gently and stir in the tahini, garam masala, soya sauce and seasonings.

5. Serve in bowls and garnish with parsley, yogurt or croutons.

LENTIL SOUP

Imperial (Metric)	American
4 oz (115g) red lentils	½ cupful red lentils
1 pint (570ml) tomato juice *or* 1 lb (455g) tomatoes, liquidized, and sufficient water to make volume	2½ cupsful tomato juice *or* 1 pound tomatoes, liquidized, and sufficient water to make volume
1 medium onion	1 medium onion
3 cloves garlic	3 cloves garlic
4 oz (115g) green lentils	½ cupful green lentils
4 tablespoonsful shoyu	4 tablespoonsful shoyu
Spring onions to garnish	Scallions to garnish
2 pints (1.1 litres) stock: vegetable water or seaweed soaking water	5 cupsful stock: vegetable water or seaweed soaking water

1. Soak the red lentils for 2 hours — this helps to sort out the small stones mixed with the red lentils.

2. Place the tomato juice, onion and garlic in a liquidizer and liquidize till smooth.

3. Place the liquid in a saucepan and add red and green lentils.

4. Simmer gently until the lentils are soft; you will need more water as the soup cooks as it thickens considerably. Make sure you stir the soup frequently to prevent the lentils sticking on the bottom of the saucepan.

5. When the lentils are cooked (you can test them by squeezing them between the thumb and third or ring finger) add the shoyu, garnish with onions (scallions) and serve immediately.

BARLEY SOUP

Imperial (Metric)	American
1 large onion	1 large onion
1 pint (570ml) vegetable stock	2½ cupsful vegetable stock
2 oz (55g) barley flakes	1¼ cupsful barley flakes
Pinch cayenne and nutmeg	Pinch cayenne and nutmeg
4 oz (115g) mushrooms	2 cupsful mushrooms
½ pint (285ml) non-fat milk	1⅓ cupsful non-fat milk
2 oz (55g) chives	2 cupsful chives

1. Peel and chop onions.

2. Sauté onions in a little vegetable stock for 5 minutes.

3. Add the barley flakes, cayenne, nutmeg and rest of stock. Simmer for 10 minutes.

4. Wipe and chop the mushrooms and add to soup.

5. Stir in the non-fat milk and cook on a gentle heat for 10 minutes. Wash and chop chives to serve as a garnish.

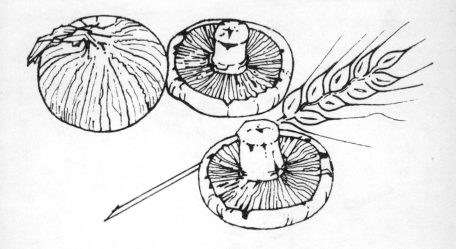

POTATO SOUP

Imperial (Metric)	American
2¼ lbs (1 kg) potatoes	2¼ pounds potatoes
4 cloves garlic	4 cloves garlic
Stock from seaweed or any vegetable water	Stock from seaweed or any vegetable water
½ teaspoonful oregano	½ teaspoonful oregano
Shoyu (naturally fermented soya sauce)	Shoyu (naturally fermented soy sauce)

1. Scrub and cube potatoes.

2. Peel and chop garlic.

3. Place the potatoes in stock and simmer. Once the potatoes boil, add oregano and garlic.

4. When potatoes are well cooked and completely disintegrated, remove from heat.

5. Add the shoyu/tamari to taste. This is replacing salt in the soup and enhances the colour.

6. Serve immediately with chopped parsley.

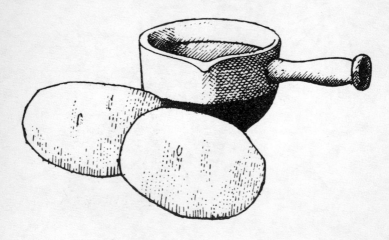

MISO SOUP

Imperial (Metric)	American
1 lb (455g) carrots	1 pound carrots
2 tablespoonsful miso	2 tablespoonsful miso
1 teaspoonful cold-pressed oil	1 teaspoonful cold-pressed oil
4 bunches spring onions	4 bunches scallions

1. Prepare the carrots by slicing diagonally and then chopping into sticks.

2. Sauté the carrot strips in a little oil. Add any type of bean or vegetable water — 1 cupful per person — and simmer gently until all the strips are tender.

3. Dissolve the miso in cold water.

4. Add enough miso to taste once the broth has been removed from the heat. *Miso should never be boiled* as this kills all of its nutrients.

5. Chop the spring onions (scallions) into small pieces to serve as a garnish.

BEAN DIP

Imperial (Metric)	American
½ lb (225g) mixed, soaked and cooked pulses	1½ cupsful mixed, soaked and cooked pulses
1 tin tomatoes	1 can tomatoes
4 oz (115g) minced onion	⅔ cupsful minced onion
2 cloves garlic	2 cloves garlic
1 teaspoonful freshly picked apple mint or ½ teaspoonful dried mint	1 teaspoonful freshly picked apple mint or ½ teaspoonful dried mint
2 tablespoonsful cider vinegar	2 tablespoonsful cider vinegar
1½ lbs (725g) fresh, wholemeal breadcrumbs	12 cupsful fresh, wholewheat breadcrumbs

1. Soak a variety of pulses. They have to be cooked together so make sure you mix pulses that have the same cooking time. As a guide, keep to pulses in one of the following groups:
    Split peas and lentils
    Small pulses, moong, aduki and whole lentils
    Kidney-shaped beans and chick peas (garbanzo beans)
    Soya beans
    Soak the pulses and cook them well. You could always use left-over cooked pulses.

2. When the pulses are cooked, liquidize them with a tin of tomatoes.

3. Mince the onion, garlic and fresh herbs and mix together with 2 tablespoonsful cider vinegar.

4. Add the breadcrumbs and onion mixture to liquidize beans and tomatoes.

5. Serve cold in the summer with raw vegetables and fruit. Serve warm in the winter with toast.

LENTIL SPREAD

Imperial (Metric)	American
4 oz (115g) whole green continental lentils	½ cupful whole green continental lentils
1 clove garlic	1 clove garlic
1 onion	1 onion
4 oz (115g) chopped mushrooms	2 cupsful chopped mushrooms
4 tablespoonsful water	4 tablespoonsful water
4 tablespoonsful shoyu	4 tablespoonsful shoyu
2 tablespoonsful cider vinegar	2 tablespoonsful cider vinegar
1 small green pepper	1 small green pepper
1 tomato	1 tomato

1. Soak lentils overnight.

2. Drain. Cover with water and simmer for 1¼ hours using approximately 2½ cupsful water to 1 cupful lentils.

3. Chop and sauté garlic and onion in water. Add chopped mushrooms for 3-4 minutes.

4. To make spread use either a fork, spoon or a blender.

5. For fork and spoon method, combine lentils and mushroom mixture with remainder of ingredients and mash.

6. For blender method, use half ingredients at a time, putting liquid ingredients into blender first. Stir in chopped green pepper, reserving a little for decoration.

7. Decorate with tomato slices and the rest of the green pepper.

8. Cool for 30 minutes before serving.

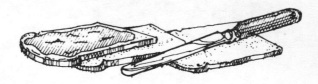

HARICOT BEAN SPREAD

Imperial (Metric)	American
4 oz (115g) haricot beans	½ cupful navy beans
1 small carton natural yogurt (low-fat)	1 small carton natural yogurt (low-fat)
Juice of 1 lemon	Juice of 1 lemon
4 sticks celery	4 stalks celery
1 bunch spring onions	1 bunch scallions
2 tablespoonsful parsley	2 tablespoonsful parsley
2 tablespoonsful toasted sesame seeds	2 tablespoonsful toasted sesame seeds
Sea salt	Sea salt

1. Soak beans overnight.

2. Drain. Cover with water, bring to boil and simmer for 1-1¼ hours using approximately 2½ cupsful water to 1 cupful beans.

3. To make spread use either fork or a blender.

4. For fork method, combine beans with yogurt and lemon and mash.

5. For blender method, use half the ingredients at a time, putting liquid, lemon and yogurt into blender first. Add finely chopped vegetables, sesame seeds and salt.

6. Decorate with sprigs of parsley and serve cold.

BUTTERBEAN AND MUSHROOM PÂTÉ

Imperial (Metric)	American
4 oz (115g) butterbeans	2/3 cupful Lima beans
4 oz (115g) mushrooms	2 cupsful mushrooms
1 onion	1 onion
1 tablespoonful tomato purée	1 tablespoonful tomato paste
1/2 oz (15g) fresh parsley	1/2 cupful fresh parsley
1 teaspoonful basil	1 teaspoonful basil
1 teaspoonful oregano	1 teaspoonful oregano
1 teaspoonful cumin seeds	1 teaspoonful cumin seeds
Juice of 1/2 lemon	Juice of 1/2 lemon
1 clove garlic	1 clove garlic
Freshly ground black pepper and sea salt	Freshly ground black pepper and sea salt
3 sticks celery	3 stalks celery
1 teaspoonful almond natural flavouring (optional)	1 teaspoonful almond natural flavouring (optional)

1. Cook beans until soft and mash with a fork.

2. Sauté vegetables in oil.

3. Add fresh parsley, herbs and spices, and continue to cook for one minute.

4. Mix all ingredients together.

5. Place into a dish and cool in refrigerator. Decorate with a sprig of parsley.

4.

BREADS AND PASTRY

CHAPATI

Imperial (Metric)
½ lb (225g) flour (this could be
  wholemeal, millet or buckwheat or
  a mixture of all three)
Pinch of sea salt
Water to mix

American
2 cupsful flour (this could be
  wholewheat, millet or buckwheat
  or a mixture of all three)
Pinch of sea salt
Water to mix

1. Mix the flour and salt.

2. Add enough water to make a stiff dough.

3. Leave to stand for 2-6 hours.

4. When the dough has stood, break it into 1½ in. (3cm) balls and knead each one individually.

5. Roll out the chapati onto a floured board until it is ⅛ in. (3mm) thick. Make sure that the dough is floured enough to stop it sticking at any time.

6. Pat the chapati between your hands, tossing it from one to the other. This gets rid of the surplus flour which is important. (If you do not do this any surplus flour will burn on the pan.)

7. Place on a dry pan to cook. It should have brown markings when cooked enough on each side.

8. Finally place the chapati onto an open flame or under the grill where it should puff.

9. Place immediately in a dry cloth. This keeps them soft.

10. You may use chapati as a bread or in place of pancakes, layered with fruit and served with maple syrup or layered with savoury fillings.

HERB BREAD

Imperial (Metric)

½ oz (15g) dried yeast or 1 oz (30g)
  fresh yeast
1 teaspoonful sweetener (honey,
  grated carrot or malt)
2 oz (55g) fresh sage or ½ the
  quantity dried sage
1 large or 2 small onions
1 lb (455g) wholemeal flour
1 teaspoonful sea salt
Liquid to mix (this could be
  vegetable stock or seaweed
  water)

American

1 tablespoonful dried yeast or
  ¼ cupful fresh yeast
1 teaspoonful sweetener (honey,
  grated carrot or malt)
2 cupsful fresh sage or ½ the
  quantity dried sage
1 large or 2 small onions
4 cupsful wholewheat flour
1 teaspoonful sea salt
Liquid to mix (this could be
  vegetable stock or seaweed
  water)

1. Dissolve yeast and sweetener in a little warm water.

2. Clean and chop the sage and onions very small.

3. In a bowl, mix together flour, salt, sage and onion.

4. When yeast is bubbling, add to flour and mix to a fruit cake consistency.

5. Lightly oil a 2 lb (1 kilo) bread tin or use a non-stick tin.

6. Place in loaf tin and leave to rise in a plastic bag.

7. When dough has reached the top of the tin, remove from plastic bag.

8. Lightly flour your fingers and poke down the edges of the dough. This gives a lovely dome shape to the bread when it is cooked.

9. Bake at 400°F/200°C (Gas Mark 6) for approximately 45 minutes.

10. Serve cold.

BASIC WHOLEMEAL BREAD

Imperial (Metric)	American
3 lb (1½ kilo) wholemeal flour	12 cupsful wholewheat flour
2 tablespoonsful cold-pressed oil (optional)	2 tablespoonsful cold-pressed oil (optional)
2 oz (55g) fresh yeast *or* 1 oz (30g) dried yeast	¼ cupful fresh yeast *or* 2 tablespoonsful dried yeast
1 teaspoonful sweetener (this could be raisin juice, water used to wash out an empty honey or jam jar, grated carrot, etc.)	1 teaspoonful sweetener (this could be raisin juice, water used to wash out an empty honey or jam jar, grated carrot, etc.)
1½ pints (850ml) liquid	3¾ cupsful liquid
1 oz (30g) salt	1 ounce salt

1. In bowls place these ingredients:

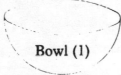

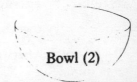

Bowl (1)   Bowl (2)

½ flour and all oil   Yeast, sweetener and liquid

2. When yeast is obviously alive by showing bubbles on the surface or a fizzing when stirred with a *wooden* spoon, mix the contents of the two bowls together to make a thick batter. Leave to rise, covered with a plastic bag or cling film.

3. When well risen, add salt and slowly add flour until you have a soft dough. You may not need all the flour at this stage — this is very important. Put your spoon down and knead the dough, introducing flour until you have a soft smooth dough. If the dough becomes hard and cracks you have made it too dry. Dry bread takes a lot of chewing and has to be stuck together with butter.

4. Shape the dough, place in an oiled tin and leave to rise until almost double in size.

5. When risen, bake at 425°F/220°C (Gas Mark 7) for 40 minutes.

LOW-FAT PASTRY
Makes ¾ lb dough (350g)

Imperial (Metric)
½ lb (225g) wholemeal flour
½ teaspoonful sea salt
½ teaspoonful baking powder
(sodium-free baking powder) *see glossary* (pages 14-16)
3 tablespoonsful cold-pressed safflower oil
Water to mix

American
2 cupsful wholewheat flour
½ teaspoonful sea salt
½ teaspoonful baking powder
(sodium-free baking powder) *see glossary* (pages 14-16)
3 tablespoonsful cold-pressed safflower oil
Water to mix

1. Mix the flour, salt and baking powder together

2. Add the oil and rub the mixture between the finger tips until it resembles breadcrumbs.

3. Mix the pastry together with enough water to form a dough.

4. Roll out very thin between two plastic bags or greaseproof paper. Use as directed.

5. Leave to stand in a cool place for 20 minutes before you cook it.

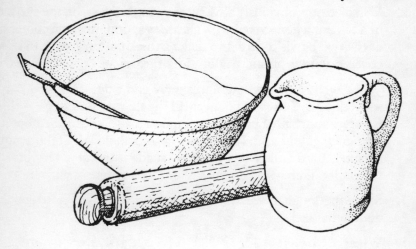

NO-FAT PASTRY
Makes ¾ lb (350g)

Imperial (Metric)
½ lb (225g) wholemeal flour
½ teaspoonful sea salt or shoyu
½ teaspoonful baking powder
(sodium-free baking powder) *see glossary* (pages 14-16)
4 oz (115g) okara
Water to mix

American
2 cupsful wholewheat flour
½ teaspoonful sea salt or shoyu
½ teaspoonful baking powder
(sodium-free baking powder) *see glossary* (pages 14-16)
4 ounces okara
Water to mix

1. Mix the flour and salt together.

2. Add baking powder and mix well.

3. Add okara (see pages 16-17 for making okara) and mix well.

4. Mix the pastry together with a little water and roll out between two plastic bags or two sheets of greaseproof paper.

5. This pastry does not keep, so cook within one hour of making.

5.

BREAKFASTS

BREAKFAST CORN
This makes a quick breakfast or sweet dish.

Imperial (Metric)	American
2 oz (55g) popping corn	1/3 cupful popping corn
Approx. 1/2 teaspoonful vegetable oil	Approx. 1/2 teaspoonful vegetable oil
Honey or rice syrup to serve	Honey or rice syrup to serve

1. Oil a pan with a well-fitting lid — use a brush and distribute the oil over the bottom to stop the grain from sticking.

2. Place the corn in the pan and immediately place on lid.

3. To stop the corn from burning, keep it moving by taking the pan off the heat and carefully shaking it or tipping the pan slightly. *Do not remove lid.*

4. The corn starts to pop once a vacuum has been created in the pan. It is very important at this stage that the corn does not burn, so make sure that you keep the pan moving on the heat.

5. When the popping has stopped take the pan from the heat and remove the lid.

6. Serve the popcorn with melted honey or rice syrup.

MUESLI

Imperial (Metric)	American
1 lb (455g) oat flakes	10 cupsful oat flakes
½ lb (225g) millet flakes or mixed flakes	5 cupsful millet flakes or mixed flakes
4 oz (115g) raisins	⅔ cupful raisins
4 oz (115g) sultanas	⅔ cupful golden seedless raisins
4 oz (115g) dates	¾ cupful dates
2 oz (55g) sunflower seeds (optional)	½ cupful sunflower seeds (optional)
2 oz (55g) sesame seeds (optional)	⅓ cupful sesame seeds (optional)
4 oz (115g) roasted and dried okara	¾ cupful roasted and dried okara

1. Mix all of the dry ingredients together.

2. Dry roast okara and when well roasted add to muesli.

Note: Muesli is much easier to digest if soaked overnight before serving. It can be soaked in any fruit juice or just water. Upon soaking the fruit becomes sweet and plump and the grain is much easier to digest. Serve with fresh fruit.

BREAKFAST CEREALS

Roasted flakes: rice
                  millet
                  oats
                  buckwheat

1. Take any combination of cereal flakes and place in a large baking dish.

2. Turn on the oven and dry roast the flakes, turning them so they all become a light brown colour. It does not matter at which temperature you roast the flakes but you have to be careful not to overcook them.

Serving suggestions:
Flakes soaked in grapefruit or orange juice are much sweeter than you imagine.
Flakes served with raisins and low-fat yogurt.
Flakes and stewed fruit.

FRUMENTARY

Imperial (Metric)	American
½ lb (225g) wheat grain	1 cupful wheat grain
3 oz (85g) fruit — dried or fresh	¾ cupful fruit — dried or fresh

1. Soak the grain and place in a dish with fresh or dried fruit.

2. Cook very slowly at 200°F/100°C (Gas Mark 3) for approx. 6 hours or overnight. A hay box would be a good idea for cooking this.

3. Serve with low-fat yogurt.

YOGURT

Yogurt starter: for low-fat yogurt you could use a low fat natural starter,
i.e. 4 tablespoonsful to 1 pint of liquid
for no-fat yogurt a commercial starter could be bought
from wholefood or health food shops
1 pint (570ml) milk: dried no-fat milk mixed with water
soya milk; see recipe for making okara (pages 16-17)

1. Heat the milk until it is at blood temperature (98.4°F), if using a cooking thermometer this is indicated as junket temperature, or test it by placing a few drops of warm milk on the back of your hand. Fingers can often tolerate extremes of heat and therefore it is not advisable to use the fingers for testing the temperature.

2. When the milk is heated mix the yogurt or yogurt culture well together.

3. Pour into sterilized containers, e.g. thermos flask or yogurt maker. If you are using a plastic or glass container, place it in a warm place. After seven hours the yogurt should be formed. To make it thicker place in the fridge for 3 hours before serving. (If the containers are not clean then your yogurt will have a bitter taste).

Note: The first lot of yogurt is always the thinnest and every batch following is usually thicker. If your yogurt separates it means it has been left too long or it has been heated to too high a temperature.

6.

MAIN COURSES

CHICK PEA AND POTATO CURRY

Imperial (Metric)	American
½ lb (225g) dried chick peas	1 cupful dried garbanzo beans
10 oz (285g) potatoes	1²/₃ cupsful potatoes
6 oz (170g) onions	1 cupful onions
1 chilli	1 chilli
1 oz (30g) fresh ginger	1 ounce fresh ginger
6 tablespoonsful water	6 tablespoonsful water
1 teaspoonful sea salt	1 teaspoonful sea salt
4 oz (115g) peas	²/₃ cupful peas
1 teaspoonful garam masala	1 teaspoonful garam masala
½ lb (225g) tomatoes	½ pound tomatoes
2 tablespoonsful fresh coriander	2 tablespoonsful cilantro

1. Soak and cook peas.

2. Wash potatoes and cut into large slices.

3. Peel and chop onions, chilli, and ginger. Add to water and simmer gently for a few minutes until onions are soft.

4. Add potatoes, sea salt, peas and further water if necessary.

5. Add the garam masala and tomatoes.

6. Simmer gently until the peas and potatoes are very soft.

7. Serve sprinkled with chopped up fresh coriander (cilantro).

GREEN PEPPER AND MISO WITH TOFU

Imperial (Metric)	American
½ lb (225g) tofu	1⅓ cupsful tofu
3 medium green peppers, 1 lb (455g) approx.	3 medium green peppers, 1 pound approx.
4 cloves garlic	4 cloves garlic
1 teaspoonful gomasio	1 teaspoonful gomasio
1 teaspoonful miso	1 teaspoonful miso
1 pint (570ml) stock (this could be vegetable water or water from soaking seaweed)	1 pint stock (this could be vegetable water or water from soaking seaweed)
1 tablespoonful honey	1 tablespoonful honey

1. Slice the tofu and grill it both sides till light brown.

2. Place a pan of water to boil.

3. Slice and clean the green peppers and place in the boiling water for 4 minutes. When the peppers have softened, place in a dish with toasted pieces of tofu.

4. Chop the cloves of garlic finely and mix with 1 teaspoonful gomasio.

5. Dissolve 1 level tablespoonful miso in a little of the stock. Add garlic and honey.

6. Add the rest of the stock and pour over tofu and peppers.

7. Cover the dish and bake for 1 hour in 325°F/170°C (Gas Mark 3).

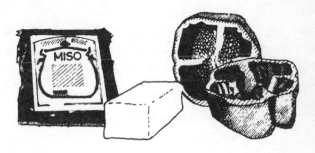

SOYA BEANS AND WAKAME STEW

Imperial (Metric)	American
4 oz (115g) dried soya beans, soaked overnight	½ cupful dried soy beans, soaked overnight
½ lb (225g) mushrooms	4 cupsful mushrooms
1-1½ tablespoonsful brown rice flour	1-1½ tablespoonsful brown rice flour
6 tablespoonsful natural soya sauce (shoyu)	6 tablespoonsful natural soy sauce (shoyu)
½ cupful dried wakame, cut into 2 in. (5cm) lengths, freshened in water and drained	⅔ cupful dried wakame, cut into 2 inch lengths, freshened in water and drained
1 carrot, diced	1 carrot, diced
2½ tablespoonsful honey	2½ tablespoonsful honey
½ teaspoonful savory	½ teaspoonful savory
½ teaspoonful cumin	½ teaspoonful cumin
½ teaspoonful coriander	½ teaspoonful coriander

1. Place beans and water into a pressure-cooker and cook for 1 hour 15 minutes.

2. Sprinkle mushrooms with 1 tablespoonful soya sauce and roll them in brown rice flour.

3. In a separate pan, heat a little water and cook the mushrooms together with any leftover brown rice flour until mushrooms are soft.

4. Pour entire contents of the pan into soya beans and quickly stir in wakame and carrot. Cook, covered, for 10 minutes, under no pressure.

5. Add remaining 5 tablespoonsful soya sauce, honey, savory, cumin and coriander and cook until beans are tender and most of the liquid has been absorbed or evaporated (about 30-40 minutes) at 10 lb pressure.

STUFFED COURGETTES

Imperial (Metric)	American
4 courgettes	4 zucchini
4 oz (115g) brown rice	½ cupful brown rice
4 oz (115g) mushrooms	4 ounces mushrooms
2 large tomatoes	2 large tomatoes
2 tablespoonsful beansprouts	2 tablespoonsful beansprouts
1 medium onion	1 medium onion
½ teaspoonful cumin	½ teaspoonful cumin
½ teaspoonful coriander	½ teaspoonful coriander
½ teaspoonful masala dal	½ teaspoonful masala dal

1. Cut each end off the courgettes and scoop out the pulp. Chop the pulp into very fine pieces.

2. Cook the brown rice in twice as much water for 25 minutes and when all of the water is absorbed, leave lid on and let it steam.

3. Chop the mushrooms, tomatoes and beansprouts finely.

4. Mix all of the ingredients together and stuff into courgettes (zucchini).

5. Place in an oiled tin and bake for 40 minutes at 375°F/190°C (Gas Mark 5).

6. Serve with tomato sauce.

Note: For this recipe choose courgettes (zucchini) which are large enough to take a teaspoon. This makes scooping out the middle easier.

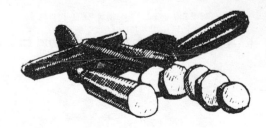

LENTIL DAAL WITH THARKA

Imperial (Metric)	American
½ lb (225g) whole lentils	1 cupful whole lentils
6 cupsful water	7½ cupsful water
2 onions	2 onions
1 teaspoonful mustard seeds	1 teaspoonful mustard seeds
1 teaspoonful turmeric	1 teaspoonful turmeric
1 green chilli	1 green chilli
1 teaspoonful coriander seeds	1 teaspoonful coriander seeds
1 teaspoonful cumin seeds	1 teaspoonful cumin seeds
1 teaspoonful garam masala	1 teaspoonful garam masala
1 teaspoonful sea salt	1 teaspoonful sea salt
1 tin tomatoes or 1 lb (455g) fresh chopped tomatoes	1 can or 1 pound fresh chopped tomatoes

1. Leave the lentils to soak overnight or for a few hours — this helps you to identify the stones and foreign bodies.

2. Clean lentils of stones and wash. Put in pan with water and bring to boil.

3. Chop the onions.

4. In another saucepan, place 1 cupful of water.

5. Bring this to the boil and add the mustard seeds, simmer for 5 minutes.

6. Add the turmeric, green chilli, coriander seeds, cumin seeds, garam masala, chopped onions, salt and tomato.

7. Mix together well and add the cooked lentils.

8. Simmer till water has become absorbed and mixture is thick.

THARKA

Imperial (Metric)	American
2 onions	2 onions
1 teaspoonful mustard seeds	1 teaspoonful mustard seeds
1 teaspoonful poppy seeds	1 teaspoonful poppy seeds
1 tablespoonful oil	1 tablespoonful oil

1. Peel and chop onions.

2. Fry onions and seeds in oil until onions are brown.

3. Pour over daal. This should be poured over when very hot and should sizzle as it mixes with the daal.

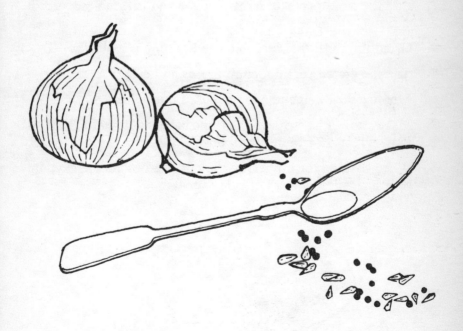

BUCKWHEAT RISSOLES

Imperial (Metric)	American
½ lb (225g) buckwheat	1 cupful buckwheat
2 oz (55g) onions, chopped	⅓ cupful onions, chopped
1 tablespoonful miso	1 tablespoonful miso
4 tablespoonsful water	4 tablespoonsful water
2 oz (55g) sunflower seeds	½ cupful sunflower seeds
4 oz (115g) grated parsnip	4 ounces grated parsnip
1 teaspoonful cumin seeds	1 teaspoonful cumin seeds
1 teaspoonful celery seeds	1 teaspoonful celery seeds

1. Roast and cook buckwheat in 2 cupsful of water. When the water has been absorbed, leave to steam with the lid on for 15 minutes.

2. Chop the onions and place in a bowl.

3. Add the tablespoonsful of miso, dissolved in 4 tablespoonsful of water.

4. Grind the sunflower seeds and add to onions and miso.

5. Add the grated parsnip, cumin seeds and celery seeds.

6. Mix together well and add to cooked buckwheat.

7. Make into burger shapes or balls and bake at 400°F/200°C (Gas Mark 6) for 35 minutes until brown.

8. When shaping the burgers, if the mixture becomes sticky, dip your hands into a bowl of cold water.

SPAGHETTI

Imperial (Metric)	American
4 oz (115g) yellow split peas	½ cupful yellow split peas
2 cloves garlic	2 cloves garlic
1 teaspoonful oregano	1 teaspoonful oregano
1 medium red pepper	1 medium red pepper
4 oz (115g) mushrooms	2 cupsful mushrooms
2 tablespoonsful shoyu	2 tablespoonsful shoyu
1 teaspoonful sea salt	1 teaspoonful sea salt
6 oz (170g) buckwheat spaghetti	1 cupful buckwheat spaghetti

1. Soak the split peas and remove any stones.

2. Cook the split peas until they disintegrate into the water. Make sure the pan does not boil dry.

3. Place a little water in a saucepan.

4. Chop and sauté garlic in the water and add the oregano.

5. Wash and chop pepper into small pieces.

6. Wipe and slice mushrooms.

7. Add chopped pepper and mushrooms to garlic.

8. Add lentils and shoyu.

To cook spaghetti:

9. Bring 3 pints (1.7 litres) of water to the boil and add salt.

10. When boiling place spaghetti in water and cook for approx. 20 minutes until soft.

11. Place the spaghetti in a dish and serve with sauce on top.

GROATS AND NUT ROAST

Imperial (Metric)	American
4 oz (115g) groats (whole oats)	⅔ cupful groats (whole oats)
4 tablespoonsful shoyu	4 tablespoonsful shoyu
1 medium onion, chopped	1 medium onion, chopped
1 teaspoonful oil	1 teaspoonful oil
4 oz (115g) mixed nuts, whole or ground, *or*	¾ cupful mixed nuts, whole or ground, *or*
4 oz (115g) okara and 1 teaspoonful almond extract	¾ cupful okara and 1 teaspoonful almond extract
2 carrots, grated	2 carrots, grated
1 tablespoonful fresh *or* ½ teaspoonful dried mixed herbs	1 tablespoonful fresh *or* ½ teaspoonful dried mixed herbs

1. Turn on oven to 375°F/190°C (Gas Mark 5).

2. Roast groats in a dry pan and cook in double the amount of water — do not stir them. It is important when cooking any grain not to stir it as it cooks from the bottom of the pan upwards. When all of the water has been absorbed, leave it to steam for 15 minutes.

3. In a wok, cook onions in oil, add nuts or okara and almond extract for 2 minutes.

4. Add cooked groats to wok together with grated carrot, shoyu and 1 tablespoonful or ½ teaspoonful dried herbs.

5. Bake in a greased dish for 1 hour.

Topping:

Slices of tomato baked on the top will make the roast moist.

Sauce:

Imperial (Metric)	American
1 tin tomatoes	1 can tomatoes
1 tablespoonful miso dissolved in a little water	1 tablespoonful miso dissolved in a little water

1. Liquidize tomatoes and heat the sauce.

2. When hot, add miso and serve immediately.

TOFU BALLS

Imperial (Metric)	American
1 lb (455g) tofu	2²/₃ cupsful tofu
½ lb (225g) spinach	½ pound spinach
2 oz (55g) sesame seeds	¹/₃ cupful sesame seeds
3 tablespoonsful shoyu	3 tablespoonsful shoyu
Soya flour	Soy flour

1. Place the tofu in a mixer and beat well. If you do not have a mixer, mash the tofu well with a potato masher.

2. Cook the spinach and mash it.

3. Grind the sesame seeds.

4. Mix together the mashed tofu, ground sesame seeds, shoyu and mashed spinach.

5. Toast the soya flour until light brown.

6. Shape the mixture into balls and roll them in the soya flour. When shaping the tofu balls, if your hands become sticky, just place them under running water — *do not* add flour.

7. Place on a non-stick tin and bake for 35 minutes at 375°F/190°C (Gas Mark 5).

Serving suggestions: Serve warm with a vegetable sauce and rice, or with sweet and sour sauce. Cold with salad.

BEAN AND RICE LOAF

Imperial (Metric)	American
6 oz (170g) mixed kidney shaped beans (pinto, flagelot, butter beans and red kidney)	1 cupful mixed kidney shaped beans (pinto, flagelot, Lima beans and red kidney)
10 oz (285g) brown rice, cooked weight	1²/₃ cupsful brown rice, cooked weight
6 oz (170g) onions	1 cupful onions
½ teaspoonful mixed herbs	½ teaspoonful mixed herbs
2 tablespoonsful shoyu or 1 teaspoonful yeast extract dissolved in 2 tablespoonsful water	2 tablespoonsful shoyu or 1 teaspoonful yeast extract dissolved in 2 tablespoonsful water
2 oz (55g) soya flour	½ cupful soy flour
4 oz (115g) mushrooms	2 cupsful mushrooms
6 tablespoonsful water	6 tablespoonsful water

1. Soak the beans for approx. 6 hours in plenty of water.

2. Cook the beans in fresh water making sure that they are well covered. Do not throw away the water, you can use it for sauces or stock. When the beans are cooked you should be able to squeeze them between the middle finger and thumb. Cooking time is approximately 35 minutes in a pressure-cooker at 15 lb and approximately 1¾ hours in a saucepan. Mash the beans when cooked.

3. Place the cooked rice in a bowl.

4. Chop the onions and add to the rice.

5. Add the mixed herbs, shoyu or yeast extract and mashed beans.

6. In a small bowl, mix the soya flour and water together. (This replaces egg as a binding agent.) Add to all the other ingredients.

7. Line a loaf tin with greaseproof paper. Very lightly oil the inside of the paper. Place ingredients in the tin and press well. Bake at 375°F/190°C (Gas Mark 5) for approximately 45 minutes until brown.

BUTTERBEAN CROQUETTES

Imperial (Metric)	American
2 oz (55g) soya flour	½ cupful soy flour
¾ lb (340g) cooked butterbeans	1½ cupsful cooked Lima beans
1 onion, finely chopped and sautéed	1 onion, finely chopped and sautéed
1 tablespoonful lemon juice	1 tablespoonful lemon juice
1 teaspoonful lemon rind	1 teaspoonful lemon rind
½ teaspoonful dried sage	½ teaspoonful dried sage
Sea salt and freshly ground black pepper	Sea salt and freshly ground black pepper
4 oz (115g) wholemeal breadcrumbs	2 cupsful wholewheat breadcrumbs
Beaten egg	Beaten egg
Tomato or courgettes for decoration	Tomato or zucchini for decoration

1. Roast the soya flour in a dry pan or under the grill until a light brown colour.

2. Soak the butterbeans (Lima beans) for 4 hours and cook them. (Approx. 45 minutes in a pressure-cooker or 1¾ hours in a saucepan with a tightly fitting lid.) To test that they are cooked sufficiently squeeze between the thumb and middle finger.

3. Peel and chop the onions.

4. Mash the beans and add the chopped onion, lemon juice, lemon rind, sage, salt and pepper, wholemeal breadcrumbs and egg.

5. Shape into croquettes and roll in the roasted soya flour.

6. Bake with sliced tomato or courgettes (zucchini) on the top.

BEAN AND BULGAR BURGERS

Imperial (Metric)	American
4 oz (115g) raw bulgar	⅔ cupful raw bulgar
4 oz (115g) kidney beans	⅔ cupful kidney beans
1 onion, sautéed	1 onion, sautéed
1 medium carrot	1 medium carrot
1 teaspoonful shoyu	1 teaspoonful shoyu
1 clove garlic	1 clove garlic
Pinch cayenne and cumin	Pinch cayenne and cumin
1 oz (30g) fresh sage *or* ½ oz (15g) dried sage	2½ tablespoonsful fresh sage *or* 1 tablespoonful dried sage
2 oz (55g) bran	½ cupful bran

1. Pour 8 fl oz (1 cupful) of boiling water on to the bulgar and leave for 20 minutes.

2. Soak the kidney beans until both sides are the same colour when split open. If there is shading within the bean then they have not been soaked for long enough.

3. Cook the beans until soft — make sure you put plenty of water in. To see if they are cooked, test them between the middle finger and thumb (approx. 1¼ hours in a pressure-cooker or 2 hours on top of the stove).

4. Peel and chop the onion.

5. Sauté the onion in a little water.

6. Grate the carrot and add to the onion.

7. Peel and chop the garlic, add this to the onion and carrot with the shoyu, cayenne and cumin.

8. Add sautéed mixture to bulgar.

9. Mash the kidney beans.

10. Chop sage and add mashed kidney beans and sage with rest of ingredients.

11. Shape the mixture into burgers and toss in bran.

12. Place on an oiled baking tray and bake at 350°F/180°C (Gas Mark 4) for approx. 40 minutes until light brown.

13. Serve with salad or stir-fry vegetables.

TOFU PIZZA

Imperial (Metric)	American
1 lb (455g) wholemeal bread dough (see page 31)	1 pound wholewheat bread dough (see page 31)
1 lb (455g) tomatoes *or* tin of tomatoes	1 pound of tomatoes *or* can of tomatoes
4 oz (115g) onions	1½ cupsful onions
1 teaspoonful dried oregano	1 teaspoonful dried oregano
1 medium green pepper	1 medium green pepper
1 egg white	1 egg white

Topping:

Imperial (Metric)	American
½ lb (225g) tofu	1⅓ cupsful tofu
2 tablespoonsful shoyu	2 tablespoonsful shoyu
1 tablespoonful mustard seed	1 tablespoonful mustard seed
½ teaspoonful turmeric	½ teaspoonful turmeric
¼ pint (140ml) stock	⅔ cupful stock

1. Roll out dough to ¼ in. (5mm) thickness and place in a non-stick tin or on a sheet of greaseproof paper (approx. 12 in. (30cm) in diameter.

2. Brush the bread dough with egg white — this stops the tomato juice making the pizza soggy.

3. If using tinned tomatoes, liquidize the tomatoes and onions together. If using fresh tomatoes, skin them by soaking in boiling water for a few minutes and liquidize them with the onions.

4. Chop the green pepper and place in a bowl of boiling water for approx. 5 minutes.

5. Mix peppers with the tomato mixture and spread on top of the bread dough.

6. Cook the tomato, onion and pepper topping by simmering for 10 minutes.

7. Make the tofu topping in a liquidizer. Crumble up the tofu and add the shoyu, turmeric, mustard seed, stock or water. You may have to add extra water to blend to a thick sauce-like texture.

8. Spoon the tofu on top of the pizza and bake at 425°F/220°C (Gas Mark 7) until the tofu is light brown. (Make sure that the tomato topping is well covered because the tofu mixture is not capable of absorbing any excess liquid.)

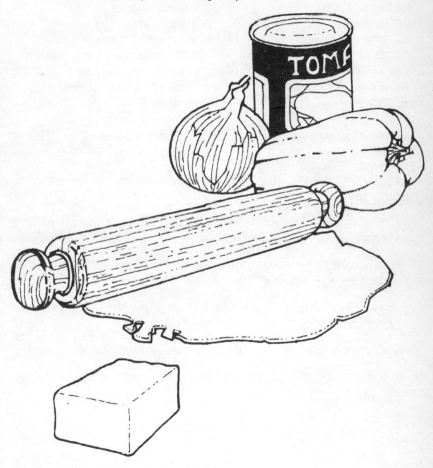

TOFU QUICHE

Imperial (Metric)	American
½ lb (225g) wholemeal pastry (use either bread dough, very thin, *or* pastry recipes on pages 32-33)	½ pound wholewheat pastry (use either bread dough, very thin, *or* pastry recipes on pages 32-33)
3 medium onions	3 medium onions
1 lb (225g) tomatoes	1 pound tomatoes
1 teaspoonful herbs	1 teaspoonful herbs
1 lb (455g) tofu	2⅔ cupsful tofu
1 tablespoonful shoyu	1 tablespoonful shoyu
½ teaspoonful home-made mustard *or* ground mustard seeds	½ teaspoonful home-made mustard *or* ground mustard seeds
½ teaspoonful black pepper	½ teaspoonful black pepper
Pinch turmeric	Pinch turmeric

1. Roll out pastry and line quiche dish approximately 9 in. (22cm) diameter.

2. Lightly fry onions and tomatoes in a little oil. Add 1 teaspoonful chopped herbs.

3. In a liquidizer place tofu, shoyu, mustard, pepper and juice from vegetables. Liquidize with enough water to make a thick sauce.

4. Add turmeric — pour onto quiche, making sure all of the vegetables are covered.

5. Bake at 375°F/190°C (Gas Mark 5) until brown at the edges and set in the middle.

6. Serve with sautéed or grilled, chopped onions on the top.

Note: Turmeric gives the tofu a yellow colour — otherwise it looks a shady brown colour.

SHEPHERD'S PIE

Imperial (Metric)	American
4 oz (115g) onions	²/₃ cupful onions
4 oz (115g) carrots	²/₃ cupful carrots
½ lb (225g) seitan	½ pound seitan
2 tablespoonsful shoyu	2 tablespoonsful shoyu
2 teaspoonsful basil	2 teaspoonsful basil
1 tin tomatoes *or* 1 lb (455g) fresh tomatoes	1 can tomatoes *or* 1 pound fresh tomatoes
2 lb (900g) potatoes	2 pounds potatoes
1 tablespoonful yeast extract	1 tablespoonful yeast extract

1. Peel and slice the onions.

2. Clean and dice the carrots into small pieces.

3. Sauté the carrots and onions in a little vegetable water or stock (e.g. seaweed soaking water) until they are tender.

4. Chop the seitan into small pieces or mince it.

5. Add the seitan to the carrots and onions. As the seitan hits the hot water it should become solid and 'behave' exactly like meat would behave in cooking.

6. Add the shoyu and basil to the seitan, carrots and onions taking care it does not boil dry. Add tomatoes and simmer for 20 minutes.

7. Boil the potatoes until very soft and mash well. Instead of putting salt with the potatoes place 1 tablespoonful yeast extract in the boiling water.

8. Place the shepherd's pie mixture in a dish and pipe the mashed potato on top.

9. Bake at 375°F/190°C (Gas Mark 5) for approx. 25 minutes until the pie is golden brown.

PASTIES

Filling:

Imperial (Metric)	American
2 leeks	2 leeks
4 oz (115g) brown rice	½ cupful (115g) brown rice
4 oz (115g) mushrooms	2 cupsful mushrooms
1 tablespoonful shoyu (soya sauce)	1 tablespoonful shoyu (soy sauce)
1 teaspoonful marjoram (dried)	1 teaspoonful marjoram (dried)

Pastry:

Imperial (Metric)	American
¾ lb (340g) wholemeal pastry (see page 33)	¾ pound wholewheat pastry (see page 33)
¾ lb (340g) wholemeal flour	3 cupsful wholewheat flour
6 oz (170g) okara (see pages 16-17 for details)	6 ounces okara (see pages 16-17 for details)
1 teaspoonful sea salt	1 teaspoonful sea salt
A little flour to roll pastry out in	A little flour to roll pastry out in

1. Wash and slice leeks and leave them to stand in a bowl of cold water.

2. Wash brown rice and cook in twice its volume of water. Cook by boiling rice until all the water has been absorbed, place on the lid and leave to steam. A total of approx. 45 minutes.

3. Wipe mushrooms and chop finely.

4. Sauté leeks, mushrooms and cooked brown rice in a little water for 5 minutes. Add the marjoram and leave to cool

5. To make the pastry place the flour, okara and sea salt in a bowl and mix well. Add enough water to make a dough. Roll out between two pieces of floured greaseproof paper. Turn the oven to 425°F/220°C (Gas Mark 7).

6. Cut the pastry into 6 in. (15cm) rounds and place filling on each one. Make into a pasty shape by bringing both sides up to the middle and pressing together. Shape the top into a wavy pattern. Traditionally this used to be the part that the tin miners in Cornwall held the pasty by. They never ate this part but just threw it away.

7. Place on an oiled tin or greaseproof paper and bake for 20 minutes. Do not wait for the pastry to brown as it will be too hard.

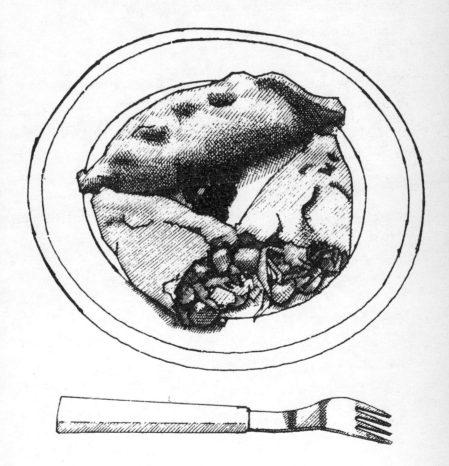

RICE GRAM DUMPLINGS

Imperial (Metric)	American
6 oz (170g) cooked brown rice	⅔ cupful cooked brown rice
2 oz (55g) gram flour	⅓ cupful gram flour
1 teaspoonful chopped parsley	1 teaspoonful chopped parsley
1 teaspoonful shoyu (soya sauce)	1 teaspoonful shoyu (soy sauce)
A little water	A little water

1. Mix the cooked rice and gram flour together.

2. Clean and chop the parsley.

3. Add the shoyu.

4. Mix all the ingredients together with a little water to make the shaping of the dumplings easier.

5. When mixed and shaped, cook for 30 minutes in vegetable water or in a vegetable stew or curry.

7.

VEGETABLES, DRESSING AND SAUCES

VINEGAR SALAD DRESSING
You can make various fat-free salad dressings by using certain herbs in vinegar, for example:

Mint
1. 4 ounces (115g) fresh mint roasted in a dry pan with no oil. Turn off the heat and add 1 pint (570ml) cider vinegar.

Chive and Basil
2. 3 ounces (85g) and 2 ounces (55g) basil roasted and placed with 1 pint (570ml) of white vinegar, either wine vinegar or rice vinegar.

Sage and Rosemary
3. 4 ounces (115g) fresh sage and 2 ounces (55g) rosemary roasted with 1 pint (570ml) rice vinegar added. Rice vinegar is a light white vinegar, very sweet compared to vinegar we know.

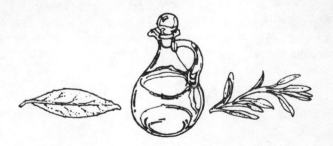

Spicy Vinegar

Imperial (Metric)	American
2 oz (55g) mustard seeds	1/3 cupful mustard seeds
2 bay leaves	2 bay leaves
2 cloves	2 cloves
Pinch nutmeg	Pinch nutmeg
Pinch asafoetida (hing)	Pinch asafoetida (hing)
Red vinegar	Red vinegar

1. Place all the ingredients in a jam jar and cover with red vinegar for 4 weeks. Strain before use.

Raspberry Vinegar

Imperial (Metric)	American
1 lb (455g) raspberries	1 pound raspberries
1 pint (570ml) red wine vinegar	2½ cupsful red wine vinegar

1. Clean the raspberries and place in saucepan with the vinegar.

2. Simmer for approx. 20 minutes.

3. Strain and bottle.

Honey and Lemon

Imperial (Metric)	American
1 tablespoonful honey	1 tablespoonful honey
2 tablespoonsful lemon juice	2 tablespoonsful lemon juice
5 tablespoonsful cider vinegar	5 tablespoonsful cider vinegar
½ teaspoonful mustard seeds	½ teaspoonful mustard seeds

1. Grind the mustard seeds.

2. Mix all of the ingredients together — use immediately.

MAYONNAISE

Imperial (Metric)	American
6 oz (170g) tofu	1 cupful tofu
6 tablespoonsful water (if you use soft commercial tofu you do not need water)	6 tablespoonsful water (if you use soft commercial tofu you do not need water)
Pinch turmeric	Pinch turmeric
1 tablespoonful lemon juice	1 tablespoonful lemon juice
1 tablespoonful mustard seeds	1 tablespoonful mustard seeds
1 teaspoonful chives	1 teaspoonful chives

1. Liquidize all of the ingredients and serve as a dip with fresh fruit and raw vegetables.

Note: Use as a salad dressing or as a dressing on cooked vegetables.

GREEN TOMATO PICKLE

Imperial (Metric)	American
2 lb (900g) green tomatoes	2 pounds green tomatoes
1 tablespoonful coriander powder	1 tablespoonful coriander powder
1 tablespoonful cumin powder	1 tablespoonful cumin powder
1 tablespoonful split mustard seeds	1 tablespoonful split mustard seeds
2 tablespoonsful cider vinegar	2 tablespoonsful cider vinegar

1. Clean and slice the tomatoes, cutting from top to bottom.

2. Mix together the coriander, cumin, mustard seeds and cider vinegar.

3. Add the sliced tomatoes and serve.

Note: This dish is lovely as an accompaniment to grain dishes and as a condiment in buffets.

MANGO PICKLE

Imperial (Metric)	American
2 lb (900g) firm, green mangoes	2 pounds firm, green mangoes
1 lb (455g) tomatoes	1 pound tomatoes
2 tablespoonsful fresh coriander	2 tablespoonsful cilantro
1 teaspoonful sea salt or gomasio	1 teaspoonful sea salt or gomasio
2 teaspoonsful cumin powder	2 teaspoonsful cumin powder
2 teaspoonsful split mustard seeds	2 teaspoonsful split mustard seeds
3 tablespoonsful wine or saki	3 tablespoonsful wine or saki

1. Clean and chop mangoes into 1 in. (2cm) pieces.

2. Clean and slice tomatoes.

3. Clean and chop coriander (cilantro).

4. Mix the mangoes, tomatoes and coriander.

5. Add salt, cumin, mustard seeds and wine.

6. Mix together well and leave to stand for 30 minutes before serving.

GARLIC, MUSHROOMS AND BUTTER BEANS

Imperial (Metric)	American
9 oz (255g) dried butter beans	1½ cupsful dried Lima beans
3 cloves garlic	3 cloves garlic
9 oz (255g) mushrooms	4½ cupsful mushrooms
½ teaspoonful sea salt	½ teaspoonful sea salt
Pinch garam masala	Pinch garam masala
2 tablespoonsful fresh, chopped coriander	2 tablespoonsful chopped cilantro

1. Soak the butter beans (Lima beans) overnight with a clove of garlic, then cook them with the clove.

2. Clean and slice the mushrooms.

3. Crush the rest of the garlic with ¼ teaspoonful sea salt.

4. Heat a non-stick frying pan or well seasoned cast iron pan.

5. Cook the garam masala in the pan with ¼ pint/140ml (⅔ cupful) of the bean water.

6. Add the butter beans (Lima beans), crushed garlic and salt.

7. Turn off the heat and add the sliced mushrooms. Place a lid on and let the mushrooms steam. This takes approximately 6-10 minutes.

Note: Serve immediately with chopped coriander (cilantro) to garnish.

ARAME SALAD

Imperial (Metric)	American
2 oz (55g) dried arame	2 ounces dried arame
1½ lb (680g) red cabbage	1½ pounds red cabbage
9 oz (225g) apples	9 ounces apples
2 tablespoonsful cider vinegar	2 tablespoonsful cider vinegar
1 clove garlic	1 clove garlic
1 teaspoonful mustard seed	1 teaspoonful mustard seed

1. Soak the arame in cold water for 10 minutes.

2. Shred the cabbage and place in bowl.

3. Grate the apples and mix with the cabbage.

4. Place the vinegar in a liquidizer with garlic and mustard seeds. Blend until smooth.

5. Mix the dressing with cabbage, apple and arame. The arame should be soft when ready to eat. Do not throw away the soaking water as this makes good stock.

Note: Arame is a seaweed and, like most seaweeds, contains many minerals that can be easily digested. It is obtainable from most wholefood shops.

RED CABBAGE SALAD

Imperial (Metric)	American
½ lb (225g) beansprouts	4 cupsful beansprouts
½ lb (225g) white cabbage	½ pound white cabbage
1 lb (455g) red cabbage	1 pound red cabbage
6 tablespoonsful raspberry vinegar	6 tablespoonsful raspberry vinegar

1. Break the beansprouts with your fingers.

2. Shred the white cabbage and mix well with the beansprouts.

3. Chop the red cabbage very finely and mix well with white cabbage and beansprouts.

4. Dress with raspberry vinegar or red wine vinegar.

Note: This would be a good salad to serve with bean dishes because the vinegar aids the digestion of beans.

MIXED GRAIN SALAD

Imperial (Metric)	American
2 oz (55g) whole wheat grain	¼ cupful whole wheat grain
2 oz (55g) whole rye grain	¼ cupful whole rye grain
2 oz (55g) whole barley grain	¼ cupful whole barley grain
1 teaspoonful sea salt	1 teaspoonful sea salt
Vegetables — green and red peppers, corn, french beans, in any quantity	Vegetables — green and red peppers, corn, french beans, in any quantity
2 cloves garlic	2 cloves garlic
1 teaspoonful honey	1 teaspoonful honey
1 fl oz (30ml) rice vinegar *or* 1 fl oz wine vinegar	2 tablespoonsful rice vinegar *or* 2 tablespoonsful wine vinegar

1. Soak the grains for 6 hours, making sure they are well covered.

2. Cook the grains in twice its volume of water plus salt.

3. Add to vegetables.

4. To prepare dressing crush the garlic and add to honey and vinegars. Shake well in a screw top jar.

5. Dress the vegetables and grains.

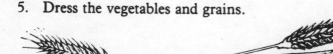

TABBOULEH

Imperial (Metric)	American
2/3 pint (340ml) boiling water	1½ cupsful boiling water
4 oz (115g) bulgar	2/3 cupful bulgar
2 cloves garlic	2 cloves garlic
4 oz (115g) chopped spring onions	2/3 cupful chopped scallions
½ lb (225g) chopped tomatoes	½ pound chopped tomatoes
2 oz (55g) chopped fresh mint (dried mint is not good in this recipe)	2 cupsful chopped fresh mint (dried mint is not good in this recipe)
2 oz (55g) chopped fresh parsley	2 cupsful chopped fresh parsley
4 oz (115g) grated carrot	4 ounces grated carrot
½ teaspoonful sea salt	½ teaspoonful sea salt
Pinch fresh ground black pepper	Pinch fresh ground black pepper
Juice of 1 lemon	Juice of 1 lemon

1. Pour the boiling water over the bulgar. Leave for 20 minutes.

2. Clean and chop the following — garlic, onions, tomatoes, mint and parsley.

3. Add the grated carrot, salt and pepper.

4. Mix all of the ingredients together.

CELERY AND WALNUT RAITA

Imperial (Metric)
6 sticks celery
2 oz (55g) chopped walnuts
¼ teaspoonful sea salt
¼ teaspoonful cayenne pepper
½ lb (225g) carton natural yogurt
  or Mayonnaise (page 61)
2 tablespoonsful fresh coriander

American
6 stalks celery
½ cupful chopped English walnuts
¼ teaspoonful sea salt
¼ teaspoonful cayenne pepper
¾ cupful natural yogurt
  or Mayonnaise (page 61)
2 tablespoonsful cilantro

1. Scrub and chop celery into very small pieces.

2. Place celery, walnuts, salt, cayenne pepper and yogurt in a bowl and mix together.

3. Serve with chopped coriander (cilantro).

ONION, TOMATO AND CHILLI SALAD

Imperial (Metric)
1 lb (455g) medium onions
1 lb (455g) firm tomatoes
½ teaspoonful sea salt
1 small chilli
1 large lemon

American
1 pound medium onions
1 pound firm tomatoes
1 teaspoonful sea salt
1 small chilli
1 large lemon

1. Peel onions, and cut into fine slices. Sprinkle with salt and leave for about ½ hour. Press out all the liquid and rinse in cold water.

2. Chop the tomatoes into small pieces.

3. Chop green chilli finely, taking out the seeds.

4. Add chilli and tomatoes to the onions.

5. Add lemon juice and stir well. Serve chilled with all types of baked vegetable, bean and grain dishes.

TAMARI ROASTED BEANS

Imperial (Metric)	American
1 medium onion	1 medium onion
4 tablespoonsful water	4 tablespoonsful water
2 tablespoonsful shoyu	2 tablespoonsful shoyu
½ teaspoonful kelp powder	½ teaspoonful kelp powder
½ lb (225g) cooked beans	1¼ cupsful cooked beans

1. Turn on oven to 350°F/180°C (Gas Mark 4).

2. Peel and slice onion.

3. Place sliced onion, water and shoyu in a liquidizer.

4. Mix the kelp powder.

5. Pour the liquidized mixture over the cooked beans and mix well.

6. Oil a baking tin very lightly.

7. Place the bean mixture into it and spread the beans out, so that none are sticking together.

8. Bake for approximately 55 minutes until all the liquid has been absorbed — take care not to burn them.

CHICORY, WALNUT AND ORANGE SALAD

Dressing:

Imperial (Metric)
2 tablespoonsful sweet cicily
3 tablespoonsful of rice or wine
   vinegar
2 cloves garlic

American
2 tablespoonsful sweet cicily
3 tablespoonsful of rice or wine
   vinegar ·
2 cloves garlic

Salad:

Imperial (Metric)
2 pieces of chicory, approx. ½ lb
   (225g)
2 oz (55g) walnuts *or* 2 oz (55g)
   cooked flagelot beans
2 large oranges

American
2 pieces of chicory, approx. ½
   pound
½ cupful English walnuts *or*
   ¼ cupful cooked flagelot beans
2 large oranges

Prepare dressing first:

1. Clean and place the sweet cicily in the vinegar. Boil for 10 minutes.

2. Liquidize the vinegar, sweet cicily and garlic together.

To prepare salad:

3. Slice and wash the chicory.

4. Chop the walnuts until the pieces are approx. ¼ in. (5mm) in size. If using flagelot beans leave whole.

5. Peel and slice the oranges.

6. Mix everything together and mix in dressing. Serve immediately.

ONION SAUCE

Imperial (Metric)	American
½ lb (225g) finely chopped onion	1⅓ cupsful finely chopped onion
1 tablespoonful shoyu	1 tablespoonful shoyu
1 teaspoonful fresh basil	1 teaspoonful fresh basil
1 tablespoonful kudzu *or* arrowroot	1 tablespoonful kudzu *or* arrowroot
1 pint (570ml) stock	2½ cupsful stock
Sea salt and freshly ground black pepper to taste	Sea salt and freshly ground black pepper to taste

1. Sauté the onions in the shoyu until soft.

2. Dry roast the basil — this can be done in a dry pan or under the grill. Add the basil to the onions.

3. Dissolve the kudzu or arrowroot in a basin with a little stock. When dissolved add the rest of the stock.

4. Add the kudzu/arrowroot stock mixture to the sautéed onions.

5. Heat gently, stirring continuously. *Note:* It is very easy for this sauce to go lumpy and thick, so do not walk away and leave it.

6. If you want a thicker sauce use more kudzu or arrowroot

7. Season to your liking and serve hot.

CARROT AND TOMATO SAUCE

Imperial (Metric)	American
1 tin tomatoes *or* 1 lb 2 oz (225g) fresh tomatoes	1 can tomatoes *or* 1 pound 2 ounces fresh tomatoes
½ lb (225g) carrots	½ pound carrots
2 tablespoonsful shoyu	2 tablespoonsful shoyu

1. If using tinned tomatoes, just liquidize them. If using fresh tomatoes, place in a bowl of boiling water for a few minutes. Use a fork or spoon to remove them and peel. Liquidize the fresh

tomatoes with ½ pint (285ml) water.

2. Clean and grate the carrots.

3. Place liquidized tomatoes in a saucepan and add the grated carrot. Simmer for approx. 20 minutes until the carrot is tender.

4. When cooked add shoyu and serve.

Note: This is a lovely sauce with rice dishes and vegetable roasts of all kinds.

TOPPINGS FOR JACKET POTATOES

Tahini, Lemon Juice and Chives

Imperial (Metric)	American
3 tablespoonsful tahini (sesame seed butter)	3 tablespoonsful tahini (sesame seed butter)
1 tablespoonful lemon juice	1 tablespoonful lemon juice
2 oz (55g) fresh chives, washed	2 ounces fresh chives, washed

1. Mix tahini and lemon juice together. When this has thickened add the clean, chopped chives.

Tomato Dressing

Imperial (Metric)	American
Small tin of tomatoes	Small can of tomatoes
1 tablespoonful shoyu	1 tablespoonful shoyu

1. Liquidize the tomatoes and place in a saucepan.

2. Simmer until half the liquid is drawn off.

3. Take off the heat and add the shoyu. Serve hot or cold.

BAKED VEGETABLES

Imperial (Metric)
½ lb (225g) parsnips
½ lb (225g) carrots
½ lb (225g) swede
A little cold-pressed oil on a brush
1 bay leaf *or* 2 curry leaves (limdo)

American
½ pound parsnips
½ pound carrots
½ pound rutabaga
A little cold-pressed oil on a brush
1 bay leaf *or* 2 curry leaves (limdo)

1. Set oven to 375°F/190°C (Gas Mark 5).

2. Wash the vegetables well. (If they are not organically grown, peel them.)

3. Very lightly oil a baking dish.

4. Grate the vegetables, mix well and place in the oven dish.

5. Place the bay leaf or the curry leaves on the top. Cover with foil.

6. Bake for approximately 25-30 minutes.

7. Serve immediately.

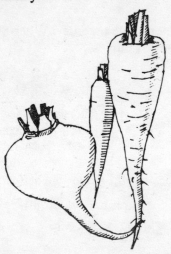

OVEN CHIPS

Imperial (Metric)	**American**
4 oz (115g) potatoes per person	4 ounces potatoes per person
Sea salt or the water from soaked seaweed	Sea salt or the water from soaked seaweed
A little oil	A little oil

1. Set the oven to 400°F/200°C (Gas Mark 6).

2. Scrub the potatoes and slice into chips.

3. Leave to soak in salt water or the seaweed water until the oven is hot.

4. Lightly oil two baking tins.

5. Dry the chips and place on baking tins.

6. Bake for approx. 30 minutes until the chips are brown. Serve immediately.

MILLET AND VEGETABLE BAKE

Imperial (Metric)	American
Vegetables — runner beans, french beans, white radish, okra, · courgettes, marrow	Vegetables — runner beans, french beans, white radish, okra, zucchini, summer squash
½ lb (225g) millet	1 cupful millet
½ teaspoonful sea salt	½ teaspoonful sea salt
½ teaspoonful garam masala	½ teaspoonful garam masala
Pinch of asafoetida (hing)	Pinch of asafoetida (hing)

1. Chop and sauté all the vegetables in a little water. Turn off the heat and leave to steam for 10 minutes.

2. Place in an oiled dish.

3. Cook the millet with the spices and salt in the cooking water.

4. Cover the vegetables with cooked millet and bake at 350°F/180°C (Gas Mark 4) for 35 minutes.

8.

CAKES AND SWEET DISHES

APRICOT MOUSSE

Imperial (Metric)	American
4 oz (115g) apricots	4 ounces apricots
1 teaspoonful cinnamon	1 teaspoonful cinnamon
4 oz (115g) tofu (Home-made or soft commercial tofu)	²/₃ cupful tofu (Home-made or soft commercial tofu)

1. Wash the apricots well and soak them in water.

2. When the apricots are well plumped, stew them in the soaking water.

3. Place the apricots in a liquidizer with 1 teaspoonful cinnamon.

4. Break up the tofu and add it to the apricots.

5. You may need to add some of the apricot cooking water to make liquidizing easier.

6. Liquidize until mixture is well blended

7. Chill before serving.

8. Serve with apricots or mandarin oranges as a garnish.

Note: The wild hunza apricots give the best flavour for this dish, but the unsulphured apricots give the best colour.

TOFU ICE-CREAM

Imperial (Metric)	American
¾ lb (340g) tofu	1⅓ cupsful tofu
8 fl oz (240ml) grape juice	1 cupful grape juice
10 black grapes	10 black grapes

1. Liquidize the tofu and grape juice together. Place in mixer bowl or large bowl.

2. Place in a deep freeze; remove after 1½ hours and whisk for 10 minutes in a mixer or by hand until it is thicker — this can take up to 20 minutes by hand.

3. Freeze again and serve with halves of black grapes.

4. Serve with Carob Sauce (pages 92-93).

Note: Tofu ice-cream is best served if it is taken out of the freezer 10 minutes before it is required.

ROSEHIP ICE-CREAM

Imperial (Metric)	American
1 heaped tablespoonful dried rosehip	1 heaped tablespoonful dried rosehip
4 cardamom pods	4 cardamom pods
¼ pint (140ml) concentrated apple juice	⅔ cupful concentrated apple juice
1 egg white	1 egg white

1. Infuse rosehip in 1 pint (570ml) of boiling water for 10 minutes.

2. Add cardamom pods.

3. Strain, and add concentrated apple juice.

4. Cool and freeze to a mush, by stirring it from time to time.

5. Beat well when almost frozen.

6. Whip 1 egg white until very stiff.

7. Mix with rosehip mixture and freeze.

YOGURT SCONES

Imperial (Metric)
½ lb (225g) wholemeal flour
½ teaspoonful sea salt
½ teaspoonful baking powder
4 oz (115g) okara
1 teaspoonful honey
¼ pint (140ml) natural low-fat
  yogurt
Honey for brushing
Poppy seeds for sprinkling

American
2 cupsful wholewheat flour
½ teaspoonful sea salt
½ teaspoonful baking soda
4 ounces okara
1 teaspoonful honey
⅔ cupful natural low-fat yogurt
Honey for brushing
Poppy seeds for sprinkling

1. Place flour and salt in a mixing bowl and sift in the baking powder.

2. Rub in the okara until the mixture resembles breadcrumbs and then stir in the honey.

3. Add the yogurt and mix to a soft dough.

4. Turn onto a floured surface, knead lightly and roll out to a ¾ in. (2cm) thickness.

5. Cut into 2 in. (5cm) rounds with a fluted cutter and place on a floured baking sheet.

6. Brush with honey, sprinkle with poppy seeds and bake in a pre-heated oven, 425°F/200°C (Gas Mark 7) for 12-15 minutes.

7. Transfer to a wire rack to cool.

AGAR JELLY

Imperial (Metric)
1 pint (570ml) of any type of fruit
   juice (preferably sugar-free)
1 teaspoonful agar-agar

American
2½ cupsful of any type of fruit juice
   (preferably sugar-free)
1 teaspoonful agar-agar

1. Boil the juice and when boiled add 1 teaspoonful agar.

2. Simmer gently for 3 minutes.

3. Leave to cool.

4. The agar should have set when cooled.

Note: You do not need a refrigerator for agar jelly to set.

Serving Suggestions:

Agar jelly and low-fat yogurt.
Agar jelly and fruit salad.

Note: Agar means to grind finely so agar-agar means very finely ground. Another name for agar is kanten. You can can buy it in powder, flakes or granules.

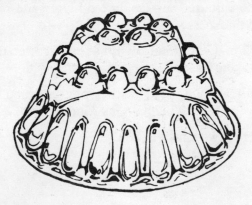

BARLEYCUP CAKE

Imperial (Metric)	American
2 eggs	2 eggs
4 oz (115g) honey	1/3 cupful honey
4 oz (115g) wholemeal flour	1 cupful wholewheat flour
1 teaspoonful sodium-free baking powder	1 teaspoonful sodium-free baking soda
1 fl oz (30ml) Barleycup	2 tablespoonsful Barleycup
Pinch sea salt	Pinch sea salt

1. Set the oven to 375°F/190°C (Gas Mark 5).

2. Whisk the eggs and honey together.

3. Fold in the flour, baking powder, barleycup and salt. *Do not beat the mixture.*

4. Oil in two 7 in. (18cm) sponge tins.

5. Place mixture in tins and cook for approx. 15-20 minutes until cake is 'springy' to touch.

6. Remove from tin and place on a wire rack to cool.

7. Sandwich together with sugar-free apricot jam.

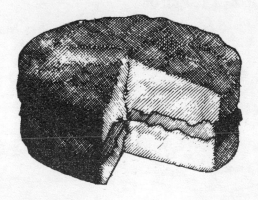

SPICE CAKE

Imperial (Metric)	American
6 oz (170g) soya flour	1½ cupsful soy flour
¾ teaspoonful cinnamon	¾ teaspoonful cinnamon
¾ teaspoonful nutmeg	¾ teaspoonful nutmeg
2 teaspoonsful sodium-free baking powder	2 teaspoonsful sodium-free baking soda
4 tablespoonsful yogurt	4 tablespoonsful yogurt
4 oz (115g) honey	⅓ cupful honey
2 oz (55g) molasses	2 tablespoonsful molasses
½ cupful low-fat or skimmed milk	⅔ cupful low-fat or skimmed milk
½ cupful water	½ cupful water
½ lb (225g) wholemeal flour	2 cupsful wholewheat flour
2 oz (55g) chopped sunflower seeds	½ cupful chopped sunflower seeds
2 oz (55g) sultanas	⅓ cupful golden seedless raisins

1. In a bowl place soya flour, cinnamon, nutmeg and baking powder.

2. Rub in yogurt.

3. Heat honey and molasses in milk with ½ cupful of water.

4. Add to flours and yogurt and mix in sunflower seeds and fruit. *Mix well.*

5. Prepare an 8 in. (20cm) tin.

6. Bake for 30-40 minutes at 375°F/190°C (Gas Mark 5).

GINGER CAKE

Imperial (Metric)	American
2 oz (55g) honey	2 tablespoonsful honey
2 oz (55g) malt	2 tablespoonsful malt
2 fl oz (60ml) water	2 tablespoonsful water
2 oz (55g) molasses	2 tablespoonsful molasses
4 oz (115g) maize flour	1/3 cupful cornmeal
4 oz (115g) gram flour	3/4 cupful gram flour
1/2 lb (225g) rice flour	1 1/2 cupsful rice flour
4 oz (115g) soya flour	3/4 cupful soy flour
1/2 teaspoonful sea salt	1/2 teaspoonful sea salt
2 cloves	2 cloves
1 1/2 teaspoonsful fresh ginger	1 1/2 teaspoonsful fresh ginger
2 teaspoonsful sodium-free baking powder	2 teaspoonsful sodium-free baking soda
1 cupful hot water	1 cupful hot water

1. Set the oven to 350°F/180°C (Gas Mark 4).

2. Heat honey, malt and water until they are well mixed and then add the molasses.

3. Stir in all of the flours, salt, cloves, ginger and baking powder.

4. Add 1 cupful of hot water.

5. Pour into an oiled 12 in. (30cm) tin and bake for 1 hour.

FRUIT RING

Imperial (Metric)	American
1 lb (455g) bread dough	1 pound bread dough
2 oz (55g) each of currants, sultanas and raisins stewed in apple juice for 20 minutes and then left to cool	⅓ cupful each of currants, golden seedless raisins stewed in apple juice for 20 minutes and then left to cool
Pinch of nutmeg and cinnamon	Pinch of nutmeg and cinnamon
Rice syrup or honey	Rice syrup or honey

1. Roll out dough to ½ in. (1cm) thick.

2. Place fruit and spices on dough and roll up, rather like a swiss roll, making sure the ends and side are sealed.

3. Shape into a ring and leave to rise. Remember it doubles in size and looks better if there is a hole in the middle when baked.

4. Bake at 400°F/200°C (Gas Mark 6) for approx. 35 minutes. The ring should be brown and still quite soft when cooked. If it is overcooked and hard, cover with a clean tea towel until it is cool. The steam will then go into the ring and soften it.

5. Brush with honey or rice syrup once out of the oven.

Note: Rice syrup is a sticky syrup, rather similar to honey and gives a sticky glaze to dough dishes. You can buy it from wholefood shops.

BANANA AND FIG CRUMBLE

Imperial (Metric)	American
4 oz (115g) figs, soaked	¾ cupful figs, soaked
3 bananas	3 bananas
4 oz (115g) dried millet, cooked	½ cupful dried millet, cooked
2 oz (55g) coconut	⅔ cupful coconut
Pinch sea salt	Pinch sea salt

1. Slice the figs and place with sliced bananas in baking dish.

2. Add enough of the soaking water to cover fruit.

3. Mix together millet, coconut and salt. Place on top of fruit.

4. Bake at 425°F/220°C (Gas Mark 7) until brown.

5. Serve with Rice Cream (page 93) or yogurt.

PUMPKIN PIE

Imperial (Metric)	American
½ lb (225g) pastry or bread dough	½ pound pastry or bread dough
3 cupsful soya milk	3½ cupsful soy milk
½ lb (225g) pumpkin purée	½ pound pumpkin paste
1 tablespoonful agar flakes or agar-agar	1 tablespoonful agar flakes or agar-agar
4 oz (115g) honey	⅓ cupful honey
½ teaspoonful each ginger, cloves and cinnamon	½ teaspoonful each ginger, cloves and cinnamon
1 teaspoonful soya flour	1 teaspoonful soy flour
2 teaspoonsful vanilla extract	2 teaspoonsful vanilla extract
1 teaspoonful grated orange or lemon peel (optional)	1 teaspoonful grated orange or lemon peel (optional)

1. Pre-heat oven to 350°F/180°C (Gas Mark 4).

2. Roll out dough or pastry case to fit a 10 in. (25cm) tin or dish, and pre-bake for 8-10 minutes.

3. Combine soya milk, pumpkin and agar in saucepan and heat almost to a boil, stirring occasionally, until agar dissolves completely.

4. Turn off heat and stir in remaining ingredients, honey, ginger, cloves, cinnamon, soya flour, vanilla extract and peel.

5. Bake for 15-20 minutes.

6. Serve with sliced peaches or apricots. Delicious either hot or cold.

APPLE AND PEAR CRUMBLE

Imperial (Metric)	American
1 lb (455g) eating apples	1 pound eating apples
1 lb (455g) pears	1 pound pears
¼ pint (140ml) apple juice	⅔ cupful apple juice
¼ teaspoonful cinnamon	¼ teaspoonful cinnamon
1 teaspoonful sweet cicily	1 teaspoonful sweet cicily
½ lb (225g) wholemeal flour	2 cupsful wholewheat flour
Pinch of sea salt	Pinch of sea salt
2 oz (55g) oats	½ cupful oats
4 oz (115g) okara	4 ounces okara

1. Wash and scrub all the fruit.

2. Chop the fruit. Do not peel. Place in a saucepan with the apple juice, cinnamon and sweet cicily and cook for 10 minutes. Place in an ovenproof dish.

3. Rub together flour, salt, oats and okara and place on fruit.

4. Cook at 375°F/190°C (Gas Mark 5) for 45 minutes.

5. Serve with Rice Cream (page 93).

LEMON GOOEY CAKE

Imperial (Metric)
1 orange
4 oz (115g) millet flour and
4 oz (115g) rice flour, *or*
½ lb (225g) dhokla flour (you can
   buy this flour ready prepared in
   Indian shops)
1 pint (570ml) low-fat yogurt (you
   can make low-fat yogurt from
   skimmed milk powder or soya
   milk)
2 tablespoonsful honey
3 tablespoonsful malt
Juice of 3 lemons
2 tablespoonsful potassium
   bicarbonate

American
1 orange
1 cupful millet flour and
¾ cupful rice flour, *or*
2 cupsful dhokla flour (you can buy
   this flour ready prepared in Indian
   shops)
2½ cupsful low-fat yogurt (you can
   make low-fat yogurt from
   skimmed milk powder or soy milk)
2 tablespoonsful honey
3 tablespoonsful malt
Juice of 3 lemons
2 tablespoonsful potassium
   bicarbonate

1. Wash and grate the orange rind and place in a bowl.

2. Mix in the flours or dhokla flour and add the yogurt.

3. Add the honey, malt and juice of 3 lemons.

4. Leave in a warm place for 24 hours.

5. Place a steamer on cooker, making sure it will hold a flat dish.

6. Oil the dish very lightly.

7. In a basin place 1 tablespoonful of sodium bicarbonate and add half the flour mixture. (This should effervesce when stirred.)

8. Place in the oiled dish and steam for 20 minutes or until set. The cake will apear moist on the surface. Repeat the process with remaining mixture.

9. On cooling, the cake sets and can be cut into small squares and served.

10. Serve cold with maple syrup.

GOOSEBERRY AND GRAPE TART

Pastry:

Imperial (Metric)
½ lb (225g) wholemeal flour
Pinch of sea salt
½ teaspoonful potassium
   bicarbonate baking powder
4 oz (115g) okara
Water to mix

American
2 cupsful wholewheat flour
Pinch of sea salt
½ teaspoonful potassium
   bicarbonate baking soda
4 ounces okara
Water to mix

Filling:

Imperial (Metric)
½ lb (225g) gooseberries
1 teaspoonful chopped sweet cicily
1 pint (570ml) apple juice
1 teaspoonful agar-agar
½ lb (225g) green grapes

American
½ pound gooseberries
1 teaspoonful chopped sweet cicily
2½ cupsful apple juice
1 teaspoonful agar-agar
½ pound green grapes

To make pastry:

1. Set oven to 425°F/220°C (Gas Mark 7).

2. Mix flour, salt, baking powder and okara together.

3. Add enough water to make a stiff dough.

4. Roll out between two sheets of greaseproof paper.

5. Line an 8 in. (20cm) flan tin or quiche dish.

6. Bake in oven for 20 minutes. There is no need to place greaseproof
   or weights in the pastry as it rarely rises.

To prepare filling:

7. Boil the gooseberries and sweet cicily in the apple juice until the

gooseberries are soft but not soggy.

8. Add the agar and stir well.

9. Simmer the gooseberry, agar and apple mixture for 4 minutes.

10. Add the grapes and leave to cool.

11. Pour into flan case and as the mixture becomes cold it will set.

DATE BARS

Imperial (Metric)	American
½ lb (225g) dates	1²/₃ cupsful dates
2 oz (55g) raisins	¹/₃ cupful raisins
3 oz (85g) sunflower seeds	³/₄ cupful sunflower seeds
1 teaspoonful cold-pressed corn oil	1 teaspoonful cold-pressed corn oil
3 oz (85g) oatmeal	³/₄ cupful oatmeal
1 oz (30g) gram flour	2¹/₂ tablespoonsful gram flour

1. Place the dates in water and cook till soft.

2. Place the raisins in water and cook till well plumped.

3. Grind the sunflower seeds.

4. Heat the oil in a pan and add oatmeal. Stir until it is a light brown colour.

5. Mix all the ingredients together.

6. Place in a non-stick tin and bake at 350°F/180°C (Gas Mark 4) for 20 minutes.

7. Cut into slices when cool.

APRICOT BARS

Imperial (Metric)	American
4 oz (115g) dried apricots	4 ounces dried apricots
½ teaspoonful orange rind	½ teaspoonful orange rind
2 teaspoonsful orange juice	2 teaspoonsful orange juice
2 oz (55g) roasted soya flour for rolling out	½ cupful roasted soy flour for rolling out
1 tablespoonful honey	1 tablespoonful honey
1 teaspoonful lemon rind	1 teaspoonful lemon rind

1. Soak the apricots in hot water till soft, approx. 10-15 minutes.

2. Grate lemon rind and orange rind.

3. Chop the apricots very finely.

4. Mix the juice and apricots together. Divide into 10 balls.

5. Roll the balls in roasted soya flour and chill for 20 minutes.

RASPBERRY AND STRAWBERRY MOUSSE

Imperial (Metric)	American
3 green cardamom pods	3 green cardamom pods
½ lb (225g) tofu (silken or regular)	1⅓ cupsful tofu (silken or regular)
½ lb (225g) strawberries	½ pound strawberries
½ lb (225g) raspberries	½ pound raspberries

1. Break open the cardamom pods and place the little black seeds in a liquidizer.

2. Break the tofu into small pieces and place in the same liquidizer.

3. Clean the strawberries and raspberries and liquidize with the tofu and cardamom pods.

4. Liquidize until the fruit is well mixed.

5. Place in individual glass dishes and chill before serving.

Note: Serve with fresh strawberries and raspberries on the top.

FRESH FRUIT CAKE

Imperial (Metric)	American
1½ lb (680g) stewed fruit including juice	1½ pounds stewed fruit including juice
½ lb (225g) raisins	1½ cupsful raisins
4 oz (115g) figs	¾ cupful figs
½ lb (225g) okara	½ pound okara
½ lb (225g) oats	2 cupsful oats
¾ lb (340g) wholemeal flour	3 cupsful wholewheat flour
½ lb (225g) sunflower seeds (optional)	2 cupsful sunflower seeds (optional)

1. Set oven to 350°F/180°C (Gas Mark 4) and lightly oil a 2 lb (1 kilo) loaf tin.

2. Mix the fruit together.

3. Add okara, oats and a little flour.

4. Mix gently as you do not want everything to become too sloppy.

5. Add remaining flour.

6. Place in an oiled tin and bake for 1½ hours.

Topping:

Imperial (Metric)	American
4 oz (115g) dates	¾ cupful dates
4 oz (115g) apple	¾ cupful apple

1. Place the dates in a saucepan and cover with water.

2. Wash and grate the apples.

3. Add the apples to the date mixture and cook until the dates are smooth. Take care the mixture does not boil dry. Add a little extra water if necessary.

4. Pipe or spread topping onto cake and serve.

SUMMER PUDDING

Imperial (Metric)	American
1 lb (455g) wholemeal flour	1 pound wholewheat loaf
1 lb (455g) stewed fruit or fresh soft fruit, e.g. raspberries or strawberries	1 pound stewed fruit or fresh soft fruit, e.g. raspberries or strawberries
Honey for spreading	Honey for spreading

1. Slice the bread into thin slices and spread with honey (there is no need to do this if you use sweet ripe raspberries or stew your fruit in apple juice prior to using).

2. Very lightly oil a 1½ pound (680g) pudding basin.

3. Arrange the slices of bread around the inside of the basin.

4. Half fill the lined basin with fruit.

5. Place a layer of bread on the top.

6. Add remaining fruit.

7. Place the remainder of the bread on top of the fruit.

8. Cover with a saucer and place a weight on top. Leave to stand in a cold place for approx. 2 hours. The pressure makes the fruit soak into the bread.

9. Turn the pudding out and serve.

Note: In winter this is a good dish to make with spicy stewed apple.

HOT FRUIT SALAD

Imperial (Metric)	American
1 lb (455g) mixed dried fruits	1 pound mixed dried fruits
2 pints (1.1 litres) apple juice	5 cupsful apple juice

1. Place the dried fruit to soak overnight in cold water.

2. Strain off the water.

3. Place the fruit and apple juice together in a saucepan.

4. Cook the fruit until soft but not soggy (approx. 20 minutes).

5. Serve hot with Rice Cream (page 93).

LOW-FAT MINCEMEAT — UNCOOKED

Imperial (Metric)	American
4 oz (115g) almonds	1 cupful almonds
½ lb (225g) currants	1⅓ cupsful currants
½ lb (225g) raisins	1⅓ cupsful raisins
½ lb (225g) sultanas	1⅓ cupsful golden seedless raisins
1 large orange	1 large orange
½ lb (225g) eating apples	½ pound eating apples
2 teaspoonsful mixed spice	2 teaspoonsful mixed spice
½ teaspoonful ground nutmeg	½ teaspoonful ground nutmeg
Orange juice	Orange juice
Brandy or rum (optional)	Brandy or rum (optional)

1. Mince almonds, dried fruit and orange.

2. Core apples and mince.

3. Add to remaining ingredients.

4. Store in a cool place.

FAT-FREE MINCEMEAT — COOKED

Imperial (Metric)	American
1¾ lb (800g) eating apples, cored and diced	1¾ pounds eating apples, cored and diced
1 lb 2 oz (500g) raisins/currants/ sultanas, washed (in any combination)	1 pound 2 ounces raisins/currants/ golden seedless raisins, washed (in any combination)
½ pint (285ml) apple juice	1⅓ cupsful apple juice
½ teaspoonful each cinnamon/ allspice/nutmeg/ginger	½ teaspoonful each cinnamon/ allspice/nutmeg/ginger
1-2 tablespoonsful miso	1-2 tablespoonsful miso
Orange and lemon peel	Orange and lemon peel
4 tablespoonsful brandy	4 tablespoonsful brandy
1 teaspoonful arrowroot or kuduzu to thicken	1 teaspoonful arrowroot or kuduzu to thicken

1. Put apples, dried fruit and apple juice in saucepan. Bring to boil then cook very slowly for 1-2 hours.

2. After 1¾ hours add the cinnamon and other spices.

3. Dissolve the miso in ¼ pint/140ml (⅔ cupful) water and add to mixture.

4. Add peel and brandy.

5. Place the teaspoonful of arrowroot or kudzu in a bowl and dissolve with a little water. Add this to the mincemeat to thicken.

Note: This mincemeat does not keep — use immediately.

CAROB SAUCE

Imperial (Metric)	American
2 oz (55g) rice flour	⅓ cupful rice flour
1 oz (30g) carob flour	¼ cupful carob flour
¾ pint (425ml) apple juice	2 cupsful apple juice
1 tablespoonful malt	1 tablespoonful malt

1. Place the rice flour and carob flour in a basin. Carob flour often becomes lumpy, so it is sometimes necessary to sieve it.

2. Mix together slowly the flours and the apple juice.

3. Place in a saucepan and gently bring to the boil, stirring all the time. Turn down the heat and simmer until the sauce thickens. If you require a thin sauce add more water.

4. When the sauce is at the required consistency add the malt. Serve hot. As the sauce cools it thickens and the thick sauce could be piped if desired.

5. If you find the texture of the sauce a little gritty, then liquidize it before serving.

RICE CREAM

Imperial (Metric)
4 oz (115g) rice flour
1½ pints (850ml) goats milk or
  skimmed milk
2 oz (55g) honey

American
¾ cupful rice flour
3¾ cupsful goats milk or skimmed
  milk
2 tablespoonsful honey

1. In a saucepan mix the honey and flour together. Add milk slowly until you have a sauce that will thicken on heating.

2. Heat the sauce gently, stirring all the time until it is the thickness you require. The longer you cook the sauce the thicker it becomes.

NO-FAT RICE CREAM

Use the same quantity of rice flour and mix with 1½ pints/850ml (3¾ cupsful) apple juice, cook as directed above — there is no need to use honey with this recipe.

FAT-FREE CHRISTMAS PUDDING
(Makes 4 × 1 lb puddings)

Imperial (Metric)	American
4 oz (115g) wholemeal flour	1 cupful wholewheat flour
½ lb (225g) wholemeal breadcrumbs	4 cupsful wholewheat breadcrumbs
½ lb (225g) currants	1⅓ cupsful currants
½ lb (225g) raisins	1⅓ cupsful raisins
½ lb (225g) sultanas	1⅓ cupsful golden seedless raisins
4 oz (115g) mixed peel (grapefruit, lime, lemon, orange)	4 ounces mixed peel (grapefruit, lime, lemon, orange)
1 oz (30g) ground almonds	¼ cupful ground almonds
4 oz (115g) stewed apples	4 ounces stewed apples
Rind of 1 lemon	Rind of 1 lemon
½ teaspoonful ground ginger	½ teaspoonful ground ginger
½ teaspoonful mixed spice	½ teaspoonful mixed spice
½ teaspoonful cinnamon	½ teaspoonful cinnamon
Pinch grated nutmeg	Pinch grated nutmeg
5 tablespoonsful okara	5 tablespoonsful okara
½ pint (285ml) ale; barley wine, etc. Guinness is excellent	1⅓ cupsful ale; barley wine, etc. Guinness is excellent
4 eggs (optional)	4 eggs (optional)

1. Place all the ingredients except eggs in a bowl and mix well together.

2. Leave to stand for 8 hours.

3. Add eggs if preferred. These are purely optional and give a more solid pudding.

4. Place in oiled basins and steam for 4 hours, or 1¼ hours at 15 lb pressure in a pressure-cooker.

5. Keep well wrapped in a refrigerator or cold place for up to 4 weeks.

Note: This is a sweet, shiny Christmas pudding.

INDEX